THE PURPOSE EXPERIMENT

6 Simple Steps to Jumpstart Your Purpose

JOY LINN MACKEY

Copyright © 2012 Joy Linn Mackey

All rights reserved. No part of this book may be used or reproduced by any means, graphic, electronic, or mechanical, including photocopying, recording, taping or by any information storage retrieval system without the written permission of the publisher except in the case of brief quotations embodied in critical articles and reviews.

ISBN: 978-1-4497-6984-0 (e)
ISBN: 978-1-4497-6983-3 (sc)
ISBN: 978-1-4497-6982-6 (hc)

Library of Congress Control Number: 2012918776

WestBow Press books may be ordered through booksellers or by contacting:

WestBow Press
A Division of Thomas Nelson
1663 Liberty Drive
Bloomington, IN 47403
www.westbowpress.com
1-(866) 928-1240

Because of the dynamic nature of the Internet, any web addresses or links contained in this book may have changed since publication and may no longer be valid. The views expressed in this work are solely those of the author and do not necessarily reflect the views of the publisher, and the publisher hereby disclaims any responsibility for them.

Any people depicted in stock imagery provided by Thinkstock are models, and such images are being used for illustrative purposes only.

Certain stock imagery © Thinkstock.

Unless otherwise indicated, Bible quotes are taken from the New International Version

Printed in the United States of America

WestBow Press rev. date: 10/16/2012

At times we may be unaccompanied, but in reality we do nothing alone in this life. Our lives always bear evidence of those whose fingerprints shape our reality.

I would like to recognize the gracious and knowledgeable team at Westbow Press for their invaluable and tireless help in bringing this book to publication. They made me feel empowered as an author and as an individual, and for that I am truly grateful.

I would like to acknowledge my sisters Deborah Ricks, Janice Harris, Leanor Hodge, and Lisa Goffe, for consistently being with me in deep and meaningful ways. There is no way I would be where I am without you. I love you dearly.

Finally, I would like to thank my dear friend Dwaine Vassell who made it his mission to become my personal coach and chief encourager concerning this book. He so willingly offered great knowledge, resources, encouragement and hope. Thank you so much my love!

Contents

Preface ix
Charge Your Expectation! xi

Chapter 1: Stop

Stop the Madness 3
Stop Thinking It's all About You 4
Stop Being a Fake 8
Stop Burying Your Head in the Sand 8
Stop Trying to Show Off 10
Stop Being Blah 11

Chapter 2: Look

Look Into the Lessons of Failure 19
Look at What the Mistakes Are Leading You To 20
Look at Your Childhood 22
Look at Who You Really Want to Be 24
Look at Your Pain 26

Chapter 3: Listen

Listen for Your New Season 37
Listen for Who You Are 38
Listen to Your Heart 41
Techniques to Help You Listen 44
To Read is to Listen 45

Chapter 4: Flex

The Self-Concept Factor	57
The Courage Factor	61
The Creativity Factor	64
The Authenticity Factor	67

Chapter 5: Rock

Rock Your Flair	75
Rock Your Faith	75
Rock Your Purpose	77
Rock Your Brilliance	78
Rock Your Financial Savvy	80
Rock Your Good Health	81

Chapter 6: Affirm

Change Your Mind	89
Change Your View of Yourself	90
Change Your View of Failure	92
Change What You Will Accept from Yourself	93
Change What You Will Create in Your Life	95

A Word on Affirmation & Visualization	101
Affirmation Cards	103
Everyday Can Be a Day at the Beach!	115
A Final Word to My Readers	119

Preface

The Purpose Experiment is a combination of my freshman work – Growing Into Your Purpose (which is now out of print) plus many of the great new things I have learned since writing that book three years ago. It presents my story as a piece of the greatest story ever told – God's story. And my hope is that you will see traces of your own story in the themes I discuss. Intertwined between the story lines are exercises and activities which will help you to capture meaning and purpose from life's experiences. Hopefully they will also teach how to maintain clarity and wholeness so that you encounter less stress and enjoy more balance and purposefulness in your life.

In this book my objective is to challenge you to live a great life. That is definitely a pretty awesome goal! However, be aware that while my definition of a great life is fun, it is not a party-filled life free of responsibility. I actually designate a great life as one where you discover precisely what you were born to be and to do. This will require some conscientiousness. It is a life where you live out your unique purpose audaciously – with a boldness that says, "I am meant to be here", because you are.

What is a purpose experiment? It is an experiment which will test your endurance, your faith, and your mental toughness. Each of us has a responsibility to use what God has deposited inside of us. If you have not explored what is inside of you, this experiment will help you to discover it. If you are already aware, this experiment will stir your motivation to use it boldly.

An experiment is an experiment because a hypothesis is being tested. A hypothesis is a theory for which the outcome is unknown, but the odds are so probable that it is worth the risk. Just think of all the wonderful possibilities of the great life you were meant to live. When you really consider it, how can you do anything else but launch your purpose experiment now? Ready, set, go!

I dare you to live a great life,

JOY LINN MACKEY

CHARGE YOUR EXPECTATION!

For plans to become more realistic, it's best to write them down. When plans are written they become more tangible, and we truly begin to expect their occurrence. It's only when our expectation and belief mechanisms are activated that our goals can become reality!

Take a few minutes to write what you are expecting to receive from this book. What are your goals? When you have completed this book what do you want to know or how do you want to feel? Lastly, what commitment are you willing to make to the process?

_____
_____
_____
_____
_____
_____
_____
_____
_____
_____
_____
_____
_____
_____
_____

Now find an accountability partner and share these expectations. Ask your partner to hold you accountable to completing the book by periodically asking you about your progress.

You can also connect with me and others who are reading this book by posting to my Facebook page at www.facebook.com/AudacityDare

Chapter 1
STOP

Hi, it's me, Joy Linn, with a few words before you begin the chapter!

Topic: STOP
There are certain habits that we just have to stop. There are certain relationships that just can't go on. And there is a certain busyness that keeps us from facing things about ourselves that just have to change. These things may have been there for a minute or what seems like a million years, but they have to go...and we know it.

As you read this portion of my story think about your life and actions with stark clarity. Be brutally honest about your motives and assess who has been in charge of your life. Has your ego or your pain usurped territory that rightfully belongs to God? And speaking of God, when was the last time the two of you spent some quality time together? If you are going to strike the oil of purpose you have to dig deep and be willing to open yourself to the truth about you. It is only in the presence of God that you will really find that. Remember - you have to face the true you before you can get to the new you!   -Joy Linn

---

Promise to Self

As I read this chapter, I promise to make a true effort to fully engage concepts that are relevant to my life.

I will assess things that may need to stop in my life, and I will walk consistently toward my God-given purpose.

_____
Sign Your Name Here

⇾ Stop the Madness

My friend, Philip, was about to get out of the car when I began pouring out the woes of yet another tragic situation in my life. During that season of my journey, most of the problems I encountered centered on money. I struggled to maintain the five-bedroom house (which I had proudly purchased with a subprime loan) as well as a luxury car, which I'd convinced myself I deserved. I was constantly trying to remain afloat in the sea of bills and debt I had incurred. Sometimes Philip would look at me as though I were a helpless child who, in a feat of independence, had gotten tangled in her blouse while trying to dress herself. The child can see no way out, but a solution is obvious to the parent.

On that day, Philip's face showed love and compassion as he looked at me. He knew that the situation that seemed so impossible to me was actually quite simple to solve. And like a parent who gently guides the shirt over his child's head, Philip gave me words that would not only free me from the tangled web I had woven, but also subsequently change my life for the better. He said, "One of the best words of advice I ever received was to do the next right thing. Do the next right thing, Joy." With that, we embraced fondly, and Philip toddled off into the summer evening dusk.

There I sat, in the car, feeling the deep meaning of that simple, yet oh-so profound phrase: *Do the next right thing*. Questions flooded my mind. I asked God how I would know "the next right thing". As I tried to quiet my thoughts and speak a simple prayer, the answer to my question became boldly evident. If I would just be quiet and spend some time alone, I would be able to make space for the holy presence of God. In those moments, I would find "the next right thing".

My life had become so loud. The voices and sounds of financial woes, job pressures, and emotional stress were drowning out the still, small voice of the Spirit. In that small moment of stillness when Philip challenged me, I discovered that "the next right thing" for me would be to encourage the presence of the Lord by spending disciplined time in a personal Bible study.

I don't remember how I came to read Matthew 21 one night soon after my God-encounter in the car. Nonetheless, it was clear as I read the verses pertaining to the parable of the wicked tenants, that the Holy Spirit was leading me to this passage for my personal study.

↠ Stop Thinking It's all About You

The parable of the wicked tenants is recorded in Matthew 21:33-46, Mark 12:1-12, and Luke 20:9-19. It speaks of a landowner who planted a vineyard and leased it out to tenants. At the time of harvest, the landowner sent servants to collect his produce from the tenants who were assigned to care for the vineyard. Instead of giving the servants what was due, the tenants beat, killed, and stoned the servants. Finally, the landowner sent his own son, thinking that they would respect him, because he was not a mere servant, he was the heir. However, much to the landowner's dismay, the tenants killed the son, also.

Since this was a parable meant to give a lesson to the listener, I began to wonder about the metaphor. Who were these characters meant to represent in real life? I wondered to whom the vineyard was given. As I dug deeper into the text, I realized that the vineyard was given to those who would accept not only the servants the landowner (symbolizing God) had sent, but also the son (Jesus) who had come to collect. The study began to transition for me from mere biblical fact to a two-edged sword (Hebrews 4:12), cutting on both sides to separate me from my lost understanding. This parable began to take life, shape, and form deep within my spirit. This was not just the story of some landowner or any landowner. This was God's story.

The Holy Spirit was prompting me into a deeper exploration of the passage's meaning to me. I began to ask myself how I fit into the story. The next thing I knew, I was no longer lying across the bed reading, I was drawing a sketch of a vineyard on the large piece of paper I had taped to the wall. First, I drew a large rectangle and separated it into parcels. Then I surmised, "If this is the vineyard, and these are the pieces leased out to each of us who believes, then what does my piece of the vineyard represent?"

As I slowly wrote my name in one of the parcels with a brightly colored marker, I pondered its meaning. It dawned on me that the piece of the vineyard with my name on it represented my life and everything that it encompassed including my body, mind, activities, relationships, and career. I then wondered if I had been guilty of killing God's Son when it was time to collect - or did I have produce to give God based on the piece of the vineyard that He has leased to me. *Leased* to me? Oh, that's right - my life is not my own. I have been bought with a price (1 Corinthians 6: 19-20). Not only is what I produce, produced for God, but I am actually His produce as well.

For many days, I made new discoveries and revelations about my life. Some of what I discovered was very difficult and tremendously hurtful. It was as if I was looking at my own reflection in a mirror. I had to face the fact that the image staring back, was indeed, mine. It was true that I had not been a good steward of the finances that God had given me. I had developed a lifestyle of "robbing Peter to pay Paul", and then borrowing again from Paul.

The realities I was forced to face were very difficult. Each time I went into prayer, I cried a river before the Lord. I could not believe I had not seen these flaws in my character. After all, I was a faithful, Holy Spirit filled, tithing, church-going Christian. I had even been in seminary for four years. As I continued a somewhat self-righteous conversation in my mind, I asked, "So, what gives?" How could I, of all people, end up being the wicked tenant in the story? The words of the prophet Isaiah came to mind. "Woe is me! I am lost, for I am a man of unclean lips, and live among a people of unclean lips; yet my eyes have seen the King, the Lord of hosts!" (Isaiah 6:5 NRSV)

Those days in the presence of the Lord began to open my understanding to what my lifestyle was saying *against* the kingdom of God I loved. Not only were my decisions hurting me, but, in many ways, they were also hurting my true witness for Christ. It was realizing that truth that provoked some stark changes in my life.

Just months prior to Philip's encouragement and my resulting study, I could not have imagined what I would do without my luxury car. Now I pondered releasing myself from the bondage it had imposed on my life. I realized getting rid of the car would be "the next right thing".

As I went through the painful yet freeing process of ridding myself of the things that had me in bondage, I knew that my house would have to be the next item to release. I began cleaning out my closets and giving items away. The more I gave away, the freer I felt. Finally, the day came when I placed my house on the market. From the day I had purchased the house, I hadn't been able to afford the monthly payments. But I had many friends at the time who were buying homes and renting out rooms for income. Buying the house seemed to be feasible. However, I soon learned that one of the quickest ways to get off track from your purpose is to turn ever so slightly away from looking at Jesus, to looking at those around you.

For me as a single woman, owning a home and being a landlord was devastating. It took all of my energy, focus, and finances. And, in the end, it took three good years that could have been spent fulfilling the greater purpose that God had for my life. Do not misinterpret what I am saying. My friends and I enjoyed very good times in that house, and the Spirit of the Lord was present. But my highest and best gifts were not being used, because the efforts to keep the house had combined with the other attending cares of this life to choke out the energy and strength to engage my God-given gifts.

You may be familiar with *The Chronicles of Narnia: The Lion, the Witch & the Wardrobe* by C.S. Lewis. It is a classic in children's literature. The story is set in the fantasy realm of Narnia. The background of the story consists of four children who are sent away to escape life during wartime. Living in a dreary, old estate the children pass the time by playing in a "magical" wardrobe cabinet. It is through this wardrobe, full of old coats, that they enter the world of Narnia. For the characters in the story, being in Narnia was a magnificent journey - resplendent and magical. But at times, it could also become very frightening.

I believe we all have times when our lives seem to take us to Narnia – a place of escape that feels real but is actually mythical. It is a place where we may battle evil like the Narnia character Aslan. Or, we may experience great encounters with God like characters Peter, Susan, Edmund and Lucy. But after our personal Narnia experience, we too must push through the coats in the wardrobe (which represent our current distractions), and emerge victorious back to the life and path from which we've veered.

There was a time in my life when I was traveling on a path full of inauthentic (mythical) endeavors. Much of what I had done in life had been based on viewing me through the eyes of others. To that point, I was acting out a script that did not represent God's true purpose for my life. I experienced a type of Narnia. Everything seemed real. But I later realized that I was merely passing the time, or on vacation, from my authentic life.

In my discovery of "the next right thing", I have experienced a breaking and a re-casting – like the resetting of a bone. For me to live an authentic life, I had to separate from the imaginary life. I could no longer pretend to be like everyone else, or do what everyone else did. I had to break away from that script and let God write a new one.

Resetting is painful, yet if the bone is not set properly, it will never heal and function the way it was designed. With respect to my life, I recognized that it would be better to take the pain and be set in God's direction than to remain as I was: functional yet crippled. The mold of my life now aligns with God's purpose and I feel whole.

While it may seem extreme for me to say that God led me to sell my house, I am convinced that it is so. First of all, God never led me to purchase a house. Therefore, the resetting process required that I sell it. Like the old coats in the Narnia wardrobe that had to be pushed aside, selling my house was "the next right thing".

↠ Stop Being a Fake

I attended a conference where Sojourners founder Jim Wallis spoke these words: "The longer you are on this journey for justice, the deeper your faith has to become." He went on to describe how our personal and communal commitments need to change. I believe Wallis' words can be applied to any journey.

How we engage in relationships, spend our time, and use our money become paramount to carrying out a genuine faith walk. What we say may be eloquent, but it is what we do that shows others who we are. Hopefully, what we say agrees with what we do, but many times that is not the case. The biblical book of James puts it this way, "Faith without works is dead." (James 2:20 NKJV) In other words, to receive salvation, and then not engage it at its truest points, depletes it of its value.

We have to really live out what we say we believe. We must move from fake-acting to faith-acting. Faith-acting is being proactive and facing life, including its challenges, fears, issues, and problems, with God-inspired confidence.

↠ Stop Burying Your Head in the Sand

Some Christians believe the biblical phrase "the battle is the Lord's" releases them from responsibility for their lives. They believe God will physically handle all of their problems. That interpretation could not be further from the truth. Instead, the phrase actually means we can take heart and take hold of our spiritual weapons to fight, knowing that God is with us. Our faith in God leads us to act and will afford us the victory.

When David spoke those words in 1 Samuel 17:47, it did not imply that he should go home and not face Goliath. Neither does it mean for us today that we should not face our life issues and problems. In fact, the scripture says David, "hastened, and ran toward the army to meet the Philistine". This text was not meant to create ostrich Christians who live with their heads in the sand. To the contrary, to become mature Christians, we must face our Goliaths – the things that taunt us and seek to tear us down - and take action against them.

For many years, my Goliath had been lust for luxury. Several years ago I remember having a deep spiritual realization of my affinity for luxury. As a budding entrepreneur I struggled with this insight, not wanting to believe that my desire for the finer things was inappropriate in God's eyes.

At the time I was a proponent of the prosperity gospel, and believed God for billionaire status. But that was not the heart of the problem. The deeper issue was my affinity for the comforts and beauties of life, beyond what I could afford. In other words, I was trying to live like a billionaire before I actually became one. Each time I hit a crisis I prayed hard, loud, stomping, clapping prayers to rebuke the devil and beg God to intervene on my behalf. When the inevitable crisis cyclone would hit, I told friends, "Yeah girl, the battle is the Lord's, and I'm standing still to see the salvation of the Lord". Meanwhile, I would never change the habits that rendered me vulnerable to crisis after crisis.

Finally, when I released (sold) my car and house, I, like David, was hastening to defeat my Goliath once and for all. I was taking action and responsibility to reconstruct my affinities. The Latin word 'finis' means border. I was now re-establishing my borders. The comforts and pleasantries I previously allowed and could not afford, I allowed no more. I was facing the truth of my financial situation, and my actions were finally beginning to agree with the lifestyle I could afford.

> **List the Hard Thing(s) You Need to Face**
>
> 1.
>
> 2.
>
> 3.

➢ Stop Trying to Show Off

I currently live in a two-room apartment on the third floor of a five-story walk up in the city. It is the smallest place I have ever lived, and, quite frankly, the least attractive. But it is the first place I have sensed a convergence of extreme peace, purpose, and freedom. I am sure much of it is because it is within my budget. I could have rented something more spacious and attractive in another neighborhood for the same price I currently pay. But after my self-discoveries and revelations, there is something special about being in a not-so-perfect apartment that brings me great relief. I think it is because there is no pretense to it. It screams, "What you see is what you get!" My new digs represent life as it really is, with cracks on the wall and a window that won't close. The tattered curtain from the previous tenant still hangs scantily in the window.

In my budding mindset of simplicity, I knew that along with an unpretentious apartment should follow an unpretentious or simple life. That is why I made the decision before moving in, to refrain from watching television for a period of time. I purposed within myself to engage prayer, study, reflection, writing, and meditation in new and deep ways. I wanted to give a sacrifice of worship to God and cleanse myself from the constant diet of media messages that had become normal in my life. It was a type of fasting and healthy self-denial.

Some years ago after ending a meat fast, I began to realize that

I was not as focused or disciplined and areas of my life began to lag. This helped me to see that fasting was a discipline, a self-denial that affected many other areas of my life in a positive way.

In Matthew 17:21 NKJV, Jesus refers to a demon that could not be cast out by the disciples. He said, "However, this kind does not go out except by prayer and fasting." I quickly came to understand that there are certain victories I cannot have if I do not make sacrifice and self-denial a part of my lifestyle. Living in my current apartment and living in simplicity are types of self-denial. These acts for me mean forgoing the affinity for luxury. It is doing the opposite of what I used to do, and re-aligning my desires. In addition, my current living situation sharpens my natural focus and spiritual keenness.

↠ Stop Being Blah

I believe that the longer we journey with God, the more deeply God calls us into the journey. Our tendency is to be excited at the beginning of a trip. We get fired up and zealous. New Christians are just that way, very zealous in the early years of their faith. Many times this happens because the church does not allow new Christians to grow at their own pace for fear of losing them. So, after some years, they lose the zeal, and the fire becomes a puff of smoke with a lot of religious rhetoric. This is not the way it is supposed to be. Ecclesiastes 7:8 NASB says, "Better is the end of a thing than its beginning." After spending time in our faith walk, we should be more and more radical for Jesus. Yes, we should realize with new understanding the depths of his teaching, and the great blessing that comes from living in Him.

I did a study some years ago on "the fear of the Lord", as the phrase is used in Psalm 111:10. A wordy, yet simple definition of "the fear of the Lord" is "a very great and unusual, more than is expected, more than people think is needed, type of respect, awe, wonder and love of God that includes admitting and submitting to His great power". It is the selling your house and your car type of unusual. It's the dance like nobody's watching type of unusual that David did when he brought back the Ark of the Covenant from

Obed-Edom's house (1 Chronicles 15:25-29). And this abnormal worship activity is not reserved for the young. It is actually what we are supposed to do when we become older and wiser in the things of God.

I believe that when God shows us something, He wants us to do something about it. There was an African Bishop who preached on several occasions at our church many years ago. We tended to laugh at him a bit. When he became energized in his sermon, and God used him to share an awesome revelation, he would get so excited that he would throw his hands in the air and yell, "Somebody, do something!" We laughed, but revelation from God was flowing in our midst. How is it that we sat there as bumps on a log rather than emitting some form of response?

So many times God shows us things, whether by natural or spiritual discernment and we offer Him no response. I think He offers it to us as a question and we take it as a statement. In other words, God will present it as if to say, "now what are you going to do about it?" Because He knows the spiritual power He has given to us, He knows that blessing will manifest if we respond. But many times we passively ignore whatever God is showing us. God may want a response as simple as praying and interceding for a situation. At other times, He may need us to take more direct action. Either way, when God shows us something, it is time for us to rise to the occasion. Somebody do something!

Chapter 1 Reminder List:
Stop self-defeating behaviors
Face your Goliath(s)
Read scripture and apply it to your life
Realize that you are a part of the greatest story ever told
Our life is not our own, it belongs to God
Press reset to get back in step with God's plan for your life
Stop being a fake
Start acting in faith
Activate appropriate levels of self-denial in your life
Zeal for God is just as much for the old as it is for the young

INVESTIGATE WHAT HAS TO STOP!

Review the list of hard things that you have to face.
Have you "spiritualized" excuses – attributed your lack of change to a spiritual reason?
Have you avoided the faith-action steps required to overcome issues in your life?
Read 1 Samuel 17. Express your thoughts and questions about the scripture in the journal section below.
Discuss your thoughts and questions with your accountability partner or other trusted friend.
Write at least 3 specific faith-action steps you will employ to face your Goliath.

_____
_____
_____
_____
_____
_____
_____
_____
_____
_____
_____
_____
_____
_____
_____
_____
_____
_____
_____
_____
_____
_____

> **TRY THIS!**
>
> *(For 3, 7, 12, or 30 days)*
>
> Go on a media cleanse. Remove television and social media and replace with prayer, Bible study, reflection, writing, meditation.

Milestone #1 Completion Checklist (check all that apply):
____I read this chapter
____I reflected on items relevant to my life
____I completed all of the activities in this chapter
____I completed the media cleanse

Be sure to keep me up to date on your progress and let me know that you have finished this chapter.

Send me a Facebook post at www.facebook.com/AudacityDare
Tweet me at https://twitter.com/AudacityDare
Email me at www. audacitydare.com/contact.html

Congratulations on Completing Milestone #1!

Enter Your Name Here

Awesomeness Trophy

Chapter 2
LOOK

I hope chapter one has begun to change your life!
Welcome to Chapter 2!

Topic: LOOK
Success is failure inside out. As frightening as it may be, you have to peel back the layers of failure in your life, and dig around on the inside, to discover the good lessons. Learning those lessons brings success.

As you enjoy this chapter, be sure to create space in your schedule for reflection. It is not enough to read my journey; you must do the inner work of looking at your own life to find clues to your purpose.   -Joy Linn

---

Promise to Self

As I read this chapter, I promise to make a true effort to fully engage concepts that are relevant to my life.

I will create space in my schedule to reflect on my journey- especially the lessons learned. I will walk consistently toward my God-given purpose.

_____

Sign Your Name Here

⤳ Look Into the Lessons of Failure

You give your best and the relationship fails. You work tirelessly and the business, though promising, becomes a washed up dream. You say a kind and helpful word, and even that is taken the wrong way. Failure hurts! It makes you feel like you are not good enough, or at least not as good as the person who seems to get it right all of the time. So you begrudge successful people their accomplishments, and with fear as your cloak you settle for less. All of this occurs because you don't allow failure to have its perfect work.

James 1:4 speaks of letting *patience* have its perfect work. As I pondered this verse I began to realize that life failures also have a work. In other words, they have a job to do that will help perfect you.

What perfect work could failure accomplish, you ask? What good could come of such pain and wasted effort? Does failure work? If so, what is its work? I pondered these questions time and time again while sitting in a puddle of my own tears, and questioning God. In these times I received spiritual assurance that the work of failure is to correct, protect, and perfect.

Failure *corrects* you by keeping you from moving further down a path that is not aligned with your God-given purpose. In whisking you away, failure opens your eyes to a new reality. Failure can also *protect* you from moving ahead with a decision that will bring permanent damage into your life. Over time, failure can work an excellence of spirit within you that will move you to higher levels of success.

Failure tests your faith, tries your patience, and builds your stamina. While it can be painful, failure can also be the greatest of blessings, if you allow it to do its work. Failure works if you allow it to teach you. It may teach you about the harsh reality of some life situations, or show you the truth of someone's intentions. It will definitely give you a look into yourself, and that's the real gem. Failure brings you a unique opportunity to open the door of success. If I had not had failed many times in business, ministry, and personal endeavors, I would not have been able to write this book.

Failure is, indeed, the admission ticket to success. But to be sure failure doesn't springboard you to success automatically. Doing so depends on how you react when you fail. If you are not willing to learn the lessons that failure teaches, then you are blocking failure from doing its work. Consequently, you are doomed to fail in a similar situation again. On the other hand, if you take the time to understand the reasons behind the failure, and change accordingly, you probably won't fail in that area again. When you let failure have its perfect work you turn the failure inside out, and let it catapult you into your success!

Finally, I became desperate. I spent concentrated time with the Lord in prayer, Bible study, meditation, and reflection. Here, in the quiet, inner journey of the Spirit, the reasons for my failure were revealed. I failed because I did not know my purpose. Not having this crucial element caused me to follow after what other people considered success. But since finding my unique purpose, I am doing what I am created to do. I am following God right into my destiny, and success has no choice but to follow after me.

⇾ Look at What the Mistakes Are Leading You To

You cannot look at a snapshot of your life and determine yourself a failure. A snapshot represents only a moment in time. You would have to assess the whole photo album in order to make a determination. Making mistakes or failing at something does not make you a failure. Many times I have personalized a failed action in my life and tried to attribute it to the nature of who I was. But this was not a correct assessment.

How can you call yourself a failure based on one encounter, one moment, or one happening? You are on a journey where there are lessons to be learned. Making mistakes is one of the ways we learn. I do not mean to imply that you have to fail at everything in order to learn anything. I am merely saying that failing does not a failure make. Because we are humans living in a fallen world, we are bound to make mistakes. The key is to make every mistake a learning and growing experience.

When I was 25, I started a gift basket business called Basket

Case. I enjoyed being creative. I thought it would be a good idea to make a little extra money using my creativity. There were quite a few things I did right with that first business attempt. There are also many things I did wrong. At the same the time I also began my first attempt at a tutoring center for children. The tutoring center was successful in the sense that I was trusted enough to have a list of clients. But, I had no real business training, and I was unable to make it successful. Since I did not have a college degree at the time, I thought going back to school would help me with these business ideas. I envisioned myself becoming the business mogul I was meant to be.

After completing my undergraduate degree, I went into the gift basket business again. I had a new name, new ideas, and a new knowledge base. I also resumed the operation of the tutoring center. Yes, I started again and ramped up a great program. I networked, received continued business training, and won first-runner up in a citywide business plan competition. Both businesses failed within five years.

A picture of one of the event displays from my now defunct centerpiece & gift basket business.

While I enjoyed the creativity that was nurtured in my life, this moment was not what my life was destined to be.

It was however a moment in time that eventually helped me to discover my true purpose.

Some years later when I was attending seminary, I got the notion to begin again with the gift basket business. When it still didn't work, I switched to creating centerpieces. I hired a graphic designer to create an exquisite image. I exhibited at events and shows. Failed, failed, and super failed. You can see why I began to see myself as a failure. I had placed all my energy and much of my creativity and know-how in ventures that continued to fail.

Exasperated and desperate I gave myself wholeheartedly to prayer, study of the Word, meditation and reflection. I gave away both of my televisions so when I came home I would not be tempted to fritter away time that could be spent hearing from God.

During this time of consecration, I understood the concept that God as my creator determines my purpose and function. You can decide to use a broom to bang on the ceiling so the residents in the apartment upstairs will quiet down. But clearly that is not how the broom was to function. The creator of the broom designed it to sweep.

Similarly, when I pursued business ideas merely to make money, or did things just because everybody else was doing it, I was not operating in the way I was designed. Those pursuits would fail because I was seeking after what I was not meant to pursue. I had not sought my creator to ask who he created me to be and how he created me to function. I had never asked, "God, what is my purpose?"

↠ Look at Your Childhood

I believe that you have always known who you were meant to be, even from the time you were a young child. While you may not have realized intellectually who you were meant to be, you certainly realized it in your sub-conscious. The things that caught your attention, the things you gravitated toward, and the things you could spend countless hours doing, were the most authentic representations of you. At that point, you did not have anyone telling you to find a career that would make the most money, or that you had to carry on the family business. And if they did tell you, you did not understand what they were saying. So you "goo-gooed" and smiled at them and returned to what you alone determined as the most interesting use of your time. Usually that was something akin to banging on a pot with a spoon.

Even as a young child, Jesus knew his purpose and pursued it. At age twelve, Jesus gave his parents the slip and spent hours in the temple. When his parents finally found him they asked how he could give them such a scare. He simply said, "Why were you searching for me? Did you not know that I must be in my Father's house?" (Luke 2:49) His parents didn't know it, but Jesus knew who he was meant to be.

When I was eight years old, I loved playing school. I made my three-year-old niece the lone student. You can imagine how difficult it was to keep a three year old seated at a desk while I wrote ABC's on the blackboard. But I actually think she liked it. I often tell my niece that she excelled in school and went on to become a lawyer because of the early education I gave her while playing school. Whether that is true or not is debatable.

But as I sat in my television-free apartment pondering these things, I came to see a definite pattern in my life. My first loves were teaching, reading, and writing. My love for these endeavors flourished through my cousin Barbara. Barbara taught elementary school when I was a child. During my days off from school, my cousin would take me with her to the school where she taught. She would let me help in the classroom. I loved visiting Cousin Barbara's class. When I was in fourth grade, she allowed me to read stories to her first grade students, and write on the board. Years later, as I worked as a university teaching assistant and was well on the path to becoming a professor, I would jokingly tell my boss, "Oh, I was a teaching assistant when I was eight".

If you take the time to think back on your early experiences, you may find many examples of people who were role models and mentors to you, and many activities that you embraced as first loves. Through those activities you can find key areas of gifting and purpose.

For instance, I find it interesting that no matter what business I operated or job position I held, I found a way to write. When I worked at the Philadelphia Stock Exchange I created a very popular employee newsletter. When I operated the tutoring business, I wrote an award-winning expansion business plan in a citywide competition. When I was heavily involved in youth ministry I wrote plays and skits for youth to perform. And even when I was in primary school, tracing and writing letters were my most favorite things to do.

List some of the activities you enjoyed as a child?
_____
_____
_____
_____
_____

⇢ Look at Who You Really Want to Be

A true self-assessment of who God made me to be (of my purpose) gave me the freedom to leave my beloved neighborhood of Germantown, releasing countless possessions. I had lived in Germantown for half of my life, the other half in Mt. Airy, just one neighborhood over. But because I was beginning to understand my purpose and what I needed in order to fulfill it, I was able to rightly judge the best environment for me. While I loved living in a familiar community with wonderful friends, I recognized that it was time for me to launch out on a solo mission. I had never lived by myself.

Was I afraid? Perhaps, but I knew that for me to unleash the books that were locked inside of me, I had to spend some time alone with God in contemplation of his plans for my life. That meant leaving what was most familiar and comfortable, for something different, foreign, and quite scary. A true appraisal also helped me to recognize that God was calling me to a "business" that was quite different from the things I had embraced previously. Finally, I had a sense of clarity. I had reached the point where I could make decisions based on purpose rather than panic.

In the past, I operated in a mode of panic and fear. I feared that I would not measure up to the expectations of others, feared I was not going to be looked at as the best and the brightest, and feared I would be looked upon as a failure. Those fears elicited panic-action, and moved me to implement numerous ideas to show others that I was always "on the brink" of something great. Those ideas ultimately failed. Whether a great place to live (I used that one a lot) or a great business, a new car or a new degree program, the panic-action was designed to throw people off the trail of recognizing I had failed. I even deceived myself into believing that the wayward actions I had embraced were the direct path to my destiny.

Once I assessed my deepest and most authentic self, I knew the direction I was headed. School was no longer a deflection tactic, but instead, a deep meaningful experience that brought me great insight and professional development. Moving to a new place satisfied the requirements of good stewardship as well as attended to the needs of my personal and spiritual development. These things no longer had to impress the world, or even me. They simply had to work well enough to allow me to carry out my daily calling.

With respect to my living space, it has taken me a while to fully embrace the importance of being functional instead of being impressive. You see, I moved from a beautiful five bedroom home into a one bedroom apartment that needed quite a bit of work. I continued to make negative comments about my apartment to friends. I remarked on its small size and shabby chic style. It took a long time (time spent in the presence of the Lord) to become comfortable with the fact that my living quarters were not the most impressive, but exactly what I needed.

I have made room for the writer, teacher, leader, thinker, and mastermind in me, to emerge. I know, and am comfortable with the fact, that I need extended quiet time alone. And I am making clearer and better decisions about how I live, work and socialize.

In my heart of hearts (by faith) I knew that I was meant to be an author, professor, and entrepreneur. Therefore, I coordinated my home, school, and work choices to benefit my future reality. Knowing my true vocation truly made me a much better decision maker.

⤳ Look at Your Pain

If I knew that I loved teaching and writing as a child, why didn't I follow that path immediately? Why do so many of us veer away from our authentic callings? As I sat in my tiny apartment in the presence of God I contemplated my life and what had become of it. I engaged the tough, emotional work of digging into the question of why.

Why did I have the need to impress people in excessive ways? I traced the source to early experiences at home and at school. In primary school, I was teased by classmates because my skin was dark. Those classmates were of the same race as me. As a child, I didn't realize that this teasing stemmed from the remnants of slavery, when lighter-skinned blacks were considered more acceptable than darker-skinned blacks. All I could grasp was that I was being teased and that meant I was unacceptable. I carried this burden alone; I didn't even tell my parents. Looking back, it was the beginning of the erosion of my self-concept.

Around the fourth grade, I started to gain weight. Until then, I had been as skinny as a rail. Noticing my weight gain, my dad started remarking that I looked like a tub of lard. Though I believe he meant no harm, my dad had no idea the effect his comments had on me. He considered himself to be joking, and I laughed along with him. However, deep down inside, I was not amused. It was then that I first learned to stuff my emotions. His teasing continued. Coupled with my experiences at school, my already fragile esteem plummeted.

I attended a new school from 5th-9th grades. The overt teasing about my skin color stopped. But in its place I experienced five years of extreme racism and prejudice by school leadership. At this predominantly white school, black students were often singled out as troublemakers, and given detention and suspension notices. It was typical of that era, and even before, for black students at my school to be singled out for "offenses" that warranted demerits whereas white students behaving in similar ways were not reprimanded. These offenses included not completing homework, chewing gum, and talking or laughing during work time.

I was a part of an accelerated program that used an educational format where students worked at their own paces. We worked in a learning center, not a classroom. Also, each student worked in her or his own cubicle to complete work. Students interacted very little with each other or the teacher, unless there were questions. It seemed to me an unnatural environment for children to have to sit for long periods without talking.

I received detention almost every week for talking in the learning center. As a result, my dad spanked me just about every week. I became frustrated and depressed. I remember once standing in my living room listening to the radio in a daze of sorts. I had a desperate prayer in my heart, I asked God if he would please fast forward beyond this time in my life. At this point in my life, it was not a surprise that I hurled myself into the hope that existed for me in Jesus Christ.

After my experience in private schools, I pleaded with my parents to allow me to attend a public high school, and they did. But was it the right choice? While it was not obvious just looking at me, it turned out that *high* school was one of the *lowest* points of my life.

In high school, I formed a fear and disdain for blacks from a lower socioeconomic class. Because very few blacks lived in the middle class Mt. Airy neighborhood where I grew up, I began to associate being black with North Philadelphia. I came to consider myself as different, and somehow not black. It was not a conscious decision. In fact, I have only become aware of it after reflecting upon it years later. However, I did consciously decide to separate myself, much like the house slave separated herself from her dark sister who worked in the fields.

When I entered public school, it was my first time encountering large numbers of poorer black people on a daily basis. I was shocked by the behavior, attitudes and actions I witnessed among blacks in the public school environment. It was true culture shock.

Before then, my only connection to this population was when my family took our Sunday drive to North Philadelphia to attend church, and to visit family. But when I entered school in a similar neighborhood, I was literally surrounded daily by a population that I had no idea how to engage.

The dress, experiences, and the style of language which the students shared were uncommon to me. And the harshness held in their faces caused me great anguish. I felt threatened, and I decided to do whatever was required, in order to survive this frightening daily experience. Yet I was grateful for after school and weekends, when I was immersed in a more familiar cultural reality.

While my friends were black, they were middle class blacks who "spoke the same language" and enjoyed many of the same things. They were friends in whose faces I hadn't seen written the hurt and pain of life. The pain and hurt that I idealized in classic black writings such as Claude Brown's *Manchild in the Promised Land*, I shunned in real life. I wondered why I was drawn to black pain in literature but was afraid of seeing it in the faces of my schoolmates.

Since primary school, I had received messages that had shaped my image of myself. My primary years taught me I was ugly, my family taught me I was fat, elementary and middle school taught me that black was bad and white was good (and I was black). The last thing I wanted to do was add being considered poor to the mix. Since in my world there were many more poor and powerless blacks than poor and powerless whites, I made the decision to be white.

By the time I became a high school senior, I constantly theorized ways to help the people whom I had encountered day after day. I mused about opening my own school, and even my own prison that would have fairer and more just practices toward prisoners. Coupled with that, I had in my mind that I would go off to college to find my white husband. Marrying someone white is not a bad desire, but for me the motivation for having this desire was rooted in an unconscious desire to withdraw from my people. I viewed having a white husband as a panacea for the ills of becoming like the poor black people I was among. In other words, I thought *marrying* white could be my ticket to *becoming* white.

What a pity! The interplay of my life during childhood and youth set me on a path to divert me from the very thing God had called me to embrace: the poor, marginalized, disenfranchised, and urban populations. While I honored activism as an intellectual ethic, I was separating myself from the very ones on whose behalf I was called to act.

You have to be just as aware of spiritual diversions as you are of spiritual blessings. The enemy of your soul knows and recognizes your purpose even when you do not. The enemy tries to thwart and abort God's calling early in your life because even when you may not recognize your power to create change, the enemy does. The evil one fears losing his evil position in the minds, hearts, and lives of the people you are called to serve.

In high school, I was given a glimpse of the pain of my people. But instead of making it a motivating force, I ran far from it. Unconsciously, I believed I had enough pain in my own life. I did not want to encounter and engage the type of pain I saw in people who seemed so different, yet were actually very much a part of me. And moreover, I surely did not want to stand in solidarity acknowledging their pain as my own.

At a time in my life when I could have embraced my purpose, I missed it, and my date with destiny was postponed. Much like the Israelites in the wilderness, I wandered. I wandered to the wrong college, wandered into the wrong marriage, and wandered into too many failed endeavors. Even though my life took different turns, it kept turning until it came back to the place God originally intended.

Chapter 2 Reminder List:
Allow failure to have its perfect work
Failure corrects, protects, and perfects
Do not personalize failure, it is not who you are
God is our Creator, he determines our purpose
You've known since a child who you were meant to be
Take the time to think back on your early experiences
Knowing your true calling will make you a better decision maker
Dig into the question, why
Be aware of spiritual diversions
Let God drive your life, He knows the way

INVESTIGATE BY LOOKING INWARD!

Examine your childhood, adolescence, and young adult years. What does your reflection teach you about who you have become? Can you pinpoint times when you felt like you were wandering? Are you still wandering?

What are the lessons that specific failures can teach you?

What is your reflection leading you to discover about the direction you are headed, or your next steps?

Write your thoughts here.

> **TRY THIS!**
>
> *Interview a few people who knew you at different stages in your life (childhood, adolescence, teen years, young adult, adult). Ask them what they remember as your key characteristics, strengths, and likes/dislikes.*

Milestone #2 Completion Checklist (check all that apply):
____I read this chapter
____I reflected on items relevant to my life
____I completed all of the activities in this chapter
____I completed the interviews

Was this chapter enlightening or interesting to you in some way? Let me know your thoughts!

Send me a Facebook post at www.facebook.com/AudacityDare
Tweet me at https://twitter.com/AudacityDare
Email me at www. audacitydare.com/contact.html

Congratulations on Completing Milestone #2!

Enter Your Name Here

Amazing You! Trophy

Chapter 3
LISTEN

I am so glad that chapter two has started you on an incredible journey of reflection! Welcome to Chapter 3!

Topic: LISTEN
Hearing and listening are two different things. To hear means to be capable, in other words, you can. To listen, however, means to make an effort to hear. It's paying attention and tuning in.

As you read this chapter be sure to tune in and make an effort to connect with yourself spiritually and emotionally. This is how you listen for clues to your purpose. You have to go beyond your mental and physical capacity and seek the deep inner resource of the Spirit. It's okay if you've never done this before. Your spiritual hearing will kick-in if you create the time and space to listen.   -Joy Linn

---

Promise to Self

As I read this chapter, I promise to make a true effort to fully engage concepts that are relevant to my life.

I will make an effort to connect spiritually and emotionally with myself and God. I will walk consistently toward my God-given purpose.

_____
Sign Your Name Here

➣ Listen for Your New Season

Sometimes I feel that I am in just the right place with God, with people, with me. I am centered and clear and right in the path of my destiny. But then, as life keeps happening I become unsure and a little frightened. I lean a bit off my axis, and the tilt makes me dizzy. It seems that when you think you have life all figured out, a new challenge comes to try you. You transition to a different place, an unfamiliar place. I think God does this to prod us to lean on Him and look to Him for the guidance we so desperately need.

I also believe God shakes things up in our lives, so that we remember to place value on the right things. So many times we place value on things that are just not that important. We are tricked into thinking certain things are important because we are around others whose values are misplaced, just as ours are. Our skewed thinking, combined with others, leaves us in a worldly place where what is wrong seems to be right, or at least acceptable. I've been through these slippery and dark places where wrong is right, down is up, and then in order to get my attention, God had to fix a fix to fix me. These days I am in constant prayer that I will value what is good, holy, lasting, and true.

When I originally thought about entering my 'second act' – the transition into the new me - I envisioned a great place where I would be shiny, bright and new. Not necessarily in a spiritual way, but you know, perfect hair and nails, tailored suits, cash flowing, and a great man to share it all with. Well, that must be act 2.5 because so far 2.0 has been a reality check. It has been a reminder to place value where value is due.

I now contend that my second act is about reaching out and grasping what is meaningful to the heart of God. It is about turning His head and causing Him to take a second glance when I walk by. It's about refocusing my attention on things that truly matter. It's simple, but it is not easy. And I can only get there if I continually listen. The only way to be a voice for God is to have my ear to His heart.

⇝ Listen for Who You Are

In our effort to please and be acceptable in the eyes of others, we place too much value and attention on things that matter little, if at all. In doing this we neglect what's truly important. Calling is important. My definition of calling is a deep spiritual desire to follow a particular occupation or line of work. For so many years I neglected to listen for my calling. I set out on my own pursuit of work, and my own endeavor to make money, but all the while I was oblivious to the call.

I think the biggest part of me that has been neglected is the writer. I have always connected to the avid reader in me. And while I had practiced journaling throughout the years, the true writer in me had been pushed aside. In the last few years, I have begun to take my eyes off of the meaningless endeavors and place more attention on hearing God. In doing this, I have become more in touch with who I really am. I realized that a major way in which I process information is through writing. At times, when I am facing a difficult decision, I start writing to see what comes out. There are other times when I cannot quite capture what I think on a particular subject. It only becomes clear as I get my pen out, and have my thoughts written and organized on paper. The written word holds deep value for me.

In 2003, quite to my surprise I became divorced. In that same year, my father, whom I loved and respected dearly, passed away. In the year that followed, I was extremely quiet. I just didn't say much. I would laugh or listen, but my words were few. My silence was very noticeable to my friends who constantly prodded me to speak. But I had nothing, absolutely nothing to say. I came to realize that the traumatic events of my life had taken an emotional toll on me causing me to lose my "voice". I didn't know who I was in the world without serving in the roles of wife, daughter or church leader.

One way God restored and assured me was through writing poetry. I remember the Sunday I wrote my first spoken word piece for Rhema Spoken Word Ministry. Writing poetry helped me break through a barrier. And when we actually performed in front of an audience, I could hear the voice of God speaking on the inside of me saying, "You are mine in the world. No one can ever take your voice again because your identity is not based on your connection with other people or even the role you play in society. Your identity is based in me and who I have created you to be. Your voice is from me and it flows through you to the world. You are called to be a voice."

A few years later I found myself having a solo retreat at the beach. I decided to take that time to really engage God around "this writing thing", as I called it. I was sheepish about sharing with people my true desire to be a writer. I felt the need to spend time seeking God's assurance that this was the road He had for me to travel.

I wrote all day and most of the night. I wrote journals, I did short creative pieces, I prayed and listened. By the time I left that vacation, I was certain I must pursue the writer's path. I encountered the Holy Spirit in that place in a new and profound way. He revealed Himself as the Writer within me.

At times, I could clearly hear the Writer's call. I would find a place, with pen in hand, to begin pouring out all that bubbled over inside of me. Beyond all doubt, I knew God was calling me to be a part of my deepest and truest self. This revelation was a major part of my purpose and how God would use me in the world. Being a voice is not merely about speaking aloud. Books also have voice, in our thoughts.

Other areas of my giftedness that had been neglected in me included the teacher, the leader and the mentor-motivator. I wondered how I would begin to understand these roles as a part of who I was created to be. I explored these areas through reading. For me, reading has been the gateway to personal growth (The bookstore is my best friend and I never met a library I didn't like). So during the year that I spent fasting from television, I committed to pray, read, journal, explore and find my most authentic self.

➤ Listen to Your Heart

As I explored my purpose, I got in the habit of celebrating the High Holy Days of Rosh Hashanah and Yom Kippur (The Day of Atonement and Jewish New Year) with a Messianic Jewish Fellowship here in Philadelphia. Messianic Jews believe in Jesus as the Messiah. Their worship of Jesus has always proven to be rich and enlightening for me as a Gentile Christian. A part of Rosh Hashanah is purposeful reflecting on your life.

I went online one year and found Rosh Hashanah reflection questions, which I loved. They helped me seriously consider my own thoughts, life, and actions. While I had always written journals and thought about my life, I had never reflected in the way these questions prompted. From here emerged the first glimpse of recovering my purpose.

The first question asked, "When do I most feel that my life

is meaningful?" My answer to this question was, "When I am engaged in deep thought and/or deep conversation". I knew enough about myself to know that while I love to laugh, fun for me also consists of engaging deeper or weightier matters. Another question asked, "What are the three biggest mistakes I've made since last Rosh Hashanah?" One of my responses was, "wasting time by not going to school".

It was this answer that placed me at the foot of my bed, crying out to God regarding what graduate degree program I should consider. You see, I had already considered three programs and had wasted much time participating in classes that were not the road to my destiny. So I kept this request before the Lord.

A few weeks later, I saw information about an open house for the Master of Organizational Leadership program. As I browsed through the course offerings, I realized that each one met a specific need I had, or area I wanted to grow in. For once I had found a program that was actually perfect for me. I started the program the next spring and graduated two years later in great awe of what God had done.

The last question worth mentioning from the Rosh Hashanah list was, "If I knew I couldn't fail what would I undertake to accomplish in my life?" My top three answers were writing a book, writing for magazines and journals, and teaching at a university. These questions guided me as I started to get to the heart of me.

I have long been a goal oriented person. I write and update goals at least three times per year. But it was not until I undertook this process of deeper reflection, and listening to my heart, that I gained insight into my true purpose. Goals are great, but without a sense of direction, they are of little value. Travelling with no direction is similar to the children of Israel who circled the same mountain for forty years, searching for their Promised Land.

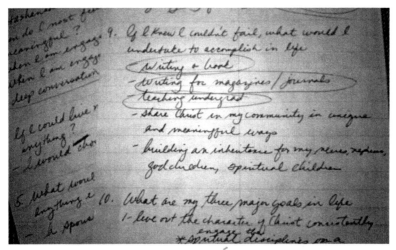

Here are my original Rosh Hashanah notes.

I have found that people who say they do not know their true purpose are not really looking for it. Like the Israelites, they are simply circling the mountain. So how does one keep from going round and round the same mountain? Well, I developed a concept called the Principle of Compounded RSAP.

To compound means to add to, to multiply, or to increase. The letters RSAP stand for reflection, self-assessment, and prayer. The formula goes like this: If you add to your time of reflection, self-assessment and prayer you are going to discover your true purpose. If you are not willing to spend time with yourself and God, you will never find your authentic self. On the other hand, if you realize the importance of living out your purpose, you will increase your quiet moments. And you will use them to reflect on what God is speaking to your heart, about who He created you to be in the world.

While the Rosh Hashanah questions were the beginning of my Compounded RSAP journey, I did not stop there. I continued to increase my times of reflection. As I adhered to this formula of adding more and more quiet reflection time to my life, in two and a half years, I was not only certain of my life's purpose, but I was operating vigorously in it.

⇸ Techniques to Help You Listen

Purpose is detected. One of the most valuable ways to start detecting purpose is through reflection on what you are called to be and do. Go to a place that you find peaceful or enjoyable (like the beach or park). Take a notebook and a pen with you to jot down important memories.

Once you are relaxed, start reflecting on your childhood. Think about moments that were special or fun. Ask yourself why you enjoyed those moments. Reflect on activities you enjoyed at various ages. Did the activities you enjoyed as a young child continue when you got older? How did they change for you as a teenager? Why did they change? What were your major accomplishments in elementary, middle and high school?

My love for and giftedness for public speaking was evident throughout my childhood. One of my fondest childhood memories was speaking to a few hundred folks at my sixth grade graduation. I felt very comfortable in that role. During high school, I won several oratorical contests. These memories connect to my most authentic calling. I loved researching for speeches as well as writing and presenting them. Besides that, others seemed to think that I did a good job. Ding, ding, ding! Enjoying something and being good at it are clues to purpose.

I also remember being bored one day, and deciding to write a play. My best friend with whom I shared the script said, "You wrote all of this?" She raved to family, friends and teachers for at least a month about the play. I actually hadn't thought much of it before her response. I was just passing the time.

As I reflected on my entire life, I realized that in most roles I assumed, writing was always in the mix. These types of memories cause you to re-discover your purpose. Take the time to recapture them and you will find gold.

The clues to my purpose unearthed during times of reflection become the substance of my prayers. I make sure that I lay my discoveries before the Lord at different times, and in various ways, to make sure that I am hearing properly and headed down the right path. I have learned the hard way not to lean solely upon my understanding of things. Instead, I allow God to direct my path. I ask God to cleanse my heart of any false pride that would cause me to think that a particular vocation is my calling, if it is not. I ask Him to clarify His thoughts and plans for me concerning new revelations I have had.

What clues to purpose do you find in your past? Maybe it was your enjoyment of using your hands to create or fix things, or helping people figure out their problems. Whatever it was, now is the time to reclaim it, redeem it, and use it to bless the world!

It is important that you always continue reflecting and searching for clues. Do not stop. You see, the value of Compounded RSAP is to keep reflecting, keep assessing yourself, and keep praying. The first few times just scratch the surface. While the first revelation will cause you to think you have found everything, it's merely a grain of sand on a vast beach. You have no idea the extent to which God wants to use the gifts within you. You have to keep digging within, and searching in the Spirit for the unique expression of your gift.

↠ To Read is to Listen

Reading is listening. When we read we have a front row seat to the thoughts and ideas of others. One of the ways I keep listening is by being an avid reader. When I read scripture and quite frankly any other book, God illuminates himself to me in very powerful ways. I buy books all day long; my home is full of them.

There are, however, a few books that I will never lend out. These are readings that have become instrumental for me in understanding my purpose. I place these on what I refer to as the bookshelf of my life. This bookshelf is composed of books that have influenced my life in amazing ways—books that I pull off the shelf year after year. The bookshelf of my life contains writings with enduring principles, insights, and anointing. I return to them to be reminded of the great refreshing they brought me in times past, and to receive new revelation I was not ready to receive during the first go-round. Here's a peek into my bookshelf.

MOTIVATION TO THE MAX!

Understanding Your Potential
Myles Munroe

Here is where it all began for me. I still remember how I felt when I first read the concepts Dr. Munroe put forth. He discussed the wealth of potential that God had planted inside of us. I poured over the book in utter amazement that God would see me as one who would affect great change in the world, for His glory. Munroe introduced me to the concepts of purpose and potential and took my breath away. This book was my entre into destiny. I would not be as passionate today about assisting you to unleash your purpose, if I had not taken the time to read this book.

Releasing Your Potential
Myles Munroe

This is the next Myles Munroe book that knocked my socks off. It's not enough to understand that you have potential; you have to learn how to release it. Dr. Munroe said, "God is the God of the impossible. But He has tied the revelation of His potential to your dreams, aspirations and prayers. That's why God is constantly challenging you to ask Him for the impossible". My goodness! Thinking about purpose in this way is simply mind-blowing. God wants His potential and His purpose to flow through you into the world. He allows you to do so through things you are good at or enjoy doing. You can't beat that with a baseball bat. It's a great deal.

The Power of Focus
Jack Canfield, Mark Victor Hansen, Les Hewitt

First of all, they call their chapters "focusing strategies". I love it! The book includes everything from habits and attitude, to confidence and persistence. Particularly influential in my life is the chapter that discusses living on purpose.

The authors encourage readers to embrace the philosophy of leaving a positive imprint on people's lives which they believe demonstrates the beginning of having a sense of purpose. This concept took the idea of purpose and yanked it up the stairs to another level. It helped me see that purpose is big and deep as well as small and simple. It taught me to engage the simple steps each day that would instantly make me a person who walks in purpose.

The Power of Focus also helped ground me in the idea of giving and serving as one of the means to discovering your purpose. This principle is one of the underpinnings of my philosophy of discovering purpose.

Seizing Your Divine Moment
Erwin Raphael McManus

This book is absolutely gripping because it takes the idea of purpose and sets it in the context of an adventure. It taught me to look at my life as a thrilling story that unfolds second by second. I think the thing that thrills me the most is that it helped me to see every moment as a fresh opportunity. We can live anew, we can make a new decision, and we can be bold and fearless!

SPIRITUAL BOOM SHAKA LAKA!

God's Favorite House
Tommy Tenney

Tenney relates the metaphor of the Ark of the Covenant in the Bible to the life of worship for believers in Christ Jesus. His insights about worship are so stunning that many times I am just dumbfounded, and propelled into worship while reading. This radical book passionately speaks of God's desire for intimate worship with His followers. It keeps me focused on being in the presence of the Lord daily, loving Him with all my heart, mind, soul and strength. I keep it right next to my Bible.

The Barbarian Way
Erwin Raphael McManus

I'm wild about Jesus and this book confirmed that I am not normal, and that this is just what God is looking for. McManus speaks about risk, passion, and sacrifice as being more aligned with a powerful faith than fitting in, following rules, and worshipping tradition. When we are each on our unique path of purpose we need encouragement like this to remind us that we were not created to be like everyone else. Get barbaric!

In the Name of Jesus: Reflections on Christian Leadership
Henri Nouwen

It is both a reminder and a challenge to Christians that living for God requires a different stance than living for what the world requires. It is a reminder that what seems right according to the world may indeed be the exact opposite of what Christ requires of us.

When I followed the leading of the Holy Spirit to sell my house and my car and move to a one bedroom apartment I so desperately needed this book. It reminded me of the heart of Christ's teaching which leads us to a life that is counter to the culture we live in. How we are to respond to Christ's teachings is expressed differently based on the unique call of God on each individual.

POWER BLAST FOR PERSONAL CHANGE!

The Success Principles
Jack Canfield

I could write a book about this book. It's 473 pages of personal change power. It is required reading in the college courses I teach. I have told countless family members and friends about it. Though I have yet to meet him, I consider Jack Canfield one of my mentors. Taking a dose of these principles each day keeps me in the right mindset for success. The bottom line is this, if you want to be successful and see personal change in your life, you must read this book. You must! You must.

The 7 Habits of Highly Effective People
Stephen Covey

This powerhouse is a staple in my life. Every single chapter is relevant. I usually include a discussion about a habit or two in most conversations with people I am coaching as well as with family and friends. After years of writing and rewriting my personal mission statement, I found the best model in Stephen Covey's book. This alone has revolutionized my life.

Second Acts
Stephen M. Pollan and Mark Levine

If you are in the midst of a life transition (or want to be) this is definitely the book to read. It served me well when I was reshaping my life. I still look to some of the exercises and stories to keep me on the path to the great life I know I am destined to live.

Once you begin to find clues to your purpose, I encourage you to begin to build your own library of books that will help you on your journey. You may consider the books I have recommended, but do not limit yourself to these. God gets our attention in different ways and through different means. So feel free to strike out on your own at the bookstore. And by all means start building your life bookshelf.

Chapter 3 Reminder List:
Listen for what is holy, lasting and true
Listen for things that are meaningful
Listen for calling...deep spiritual desire for a type of work
Listen to your past, present and future
Listen in prayer
Listen for what's most authentically you
Listen to your times of reflection and self-assessment
Listen to what you enjoy doing and do well
Listen to inspirational books
Listen

INVESTIGATE BY REFLECTIVE LISTENING!

Read the three Rosh Hashanah question below. Pray. Reflect. Now thoughtfully answer the questions.

1) *When do you most feel that your life is meaningful?*

_____
_____
_____
_____
_____
_____

2) *What are the three biggest mistakes you have made in the last year?*

_____
_____
_____
_____
_____
_____

3) *If you knew you couldn't fail what would you undertake to accomplish in your life?*

_____
_____
_____
_____
_____
_____
_____

> **TRY THIS!**
>
> Take a half hour, a half day or a weekend for a solo retreat. Relax and take time to read, pray, reflect, self-assess, and journal. Listen.

Milestone #3 Completion Checklist (check all that apply):
____I read this chapter
____I reflected on items relevant to my life
____I completed all of the activities in this chapter
____I completed the solo retreat

Feel free to ask me any questions you would like.
I look forward to hearing from you today!

Send me a Facebook post at www.facebook.com/AudacityDare
Tweet me at https://twitter.com/AudacityDare
Email me at www. audacitydare.com/contact.html

Congratulations on Completing Milestone #3!

Enter Your Name Here

You're So Phenomenal! Trophy

Chapter 4
FLEX

I am positive that chapter three has given you great new insight about your life! <u>Welcome to Chapter 4</u>

Topic: FLEX
Living intentionally with purpose is a whole new chapter in our lives! It's time to flex the muscles of great new habits. We have to "work out" – live out - new practices in order to see the successful results we desire.

Connect deeply to this chapter by implementing all of the factors into your life – good self concept, courage, creativity, authenticity. If you already work these muscles, take it to the next level of intensity. Ok, ready, FLEX! —Joy Linn

---

Promise to Self

As I read this chapter, I promise to make a true effort to fully engage concepts that are relevant to my life.

I will integrate 1-2 new positive habits into my life. I will walk consistently toward my God-given purpose.

_____

Sign Your Name Here

➤ The Self-Concept Factor

I am brilliant, creative and unique. The ability to change and influence the world is within my reach. I am not Albert Einstein or Thomas Edison, but the purpose I hold is one of a kind, unparalleled, and extraordinary. I am designed to be great, and to do phenomenal things. When I truly believe this I am at my best. When I don't, I stumble toward something less.

We tend to fluctuate about what we believe about ourselves, and sometimes even give our thoughts over to ineffective scripts that parrot old paradigms. As Christians, why do we find it so hard to believe in ourselves? I think it boils down to three reasons; what we believe about God; who we spend the most time with; and how we choose to direct our thoughts and energy.

Christians are taught to place their confidence in God, but does that mean that we are not meant to be people who possess a healthy self-concept? There are scriptures (like Philippians 3:3) which tell us not to place our confidence "in the flesh", but instead, to place our trust in Christ. In other words, our dependence should not lie in our natural abilities or advantages. Instead, we must recognize the true source of these things as Christ, and place our trust in Him.

These teachings help to remind us that we are not the masters of our own fate. There is One greater than humanity and all of life, our Creator. But how does this relate to personal self-concept? Does humbling ourselves before God mean that we do not live among humanity with the realization of the greatness placed within us? I think Jesus had an uncanny awareness of his greatness, yet he was the most humble man that ever lived.

The words *confidence* and *self-concept* are many times used interchangeably. But these two ideas actually have different meanings. Some Christians believe that the idea of having, "no confidence in the flesh", is equal to having a mediocre perception of self. But I don't think that God is asking us to put ourselves down, or think less of ourselves.

According to the online Google dictionary, *confidence* is a feeling of self assurance arising from one's appreciation of one's own abilities or qualities. *Self concept* on the other hand, is an idea of the self, constructed from the *beliefs* one holds about oneself. There is an important distinction between these two words. *Self-concept* is based in "beliefs". *Confidence* is based in our "self assurance" and "abilities".

I do appreciate my abilities and the qualities about myself, but I do not receive my security –assurance - from them. Therefore, I understand how scripture could say that we should have "no *confidence*" in the flesh – no self assurance based in our abilities. But, if my belief about myself comes from a holistic view of scripture, then Christ is my assurance, security, and stability. Therefore, I should have a *positive* self concept, and think well of myself.

Yes, I believe God wants us to have a positive self concept. In the book of Genesis, we (human beings) are listed as the crowning achievement of God's creative efforts. At intervals during creation, God paused, looked, and said, "It is good" (Genesis 1:4, 10, 12, 18, 21, 25). After adding humanity to the mix he paused, looked, and said, "It is *very* good" (Genesis 1:31).

God gave us his own image, his own breath, and even a realm where we have authority to rule. I think it's safe to say that we placed high on the value scale. To belittle ourselves or think that we have little worth is to insult God. Growing into our purpose is about believing what *God* says about us.

We are not cocky or conceited, nor do we have an over exaggerated sense of our importance. But we do know our value and our worth. In this new chapter we must take time to gain deeper understanding about what we believe about God, so that we have power to accomplish the mission at hand.

I also think we find it hard to believe in ourselves because of the people and environments we are around. When I first heard the concept that we are the average of the five people we spend the most time with, I was shocked. I surely did not wish to be the average of the people I was hanging around with at the time. And while this statement is not a hard and fast or absolute rule, I do think it has some validity.

During our lifetime, hopefully, we are able to have at least a few really fun, healthy, uplifting relationships. But the reality is, we come in contact with many types of people. And many times they are not the happiest people to endure. I am referring to those people in our lives who are negative, lazy, fearful, unfocused, procrastinators, pessimists, etc. Depending on the level and intensity of their poor attitude and behavior, these people can actually be toxic. The danger is in how their ways can drain us of what we need for a vibrant life. Many times we don't believe in ourselves because the people around us don't want the best for us. Here are some characteristics of toxic people:

- They bring us down spiritually and emotionally
- They make fun of our hopes and dreams
- They don't readily help us
- They don't want to do anything and encourage us to do nothing as well
- They tell us we can't

-OR-

- They only want to gossip, not have purpose based conversations
- They are educated or talented but never move forward
- They say they want to accomplish goals but never take action
- They have a defeatist or worrier perspective about most things
- They dilly dally their way through life

These two sets of characteristics differ but they have the same outcome. The person is stuck and wants us to stay trapped with them. Depending on the closeness of the relationship we may find ourselves doing just that. At this point we have believed more in that person than in ourselves. If we want to unleash our brilliance, we must find strength to break away from toxic relationships. This new chapter is about being free to soar. We must surround ourselves with positive people who are headed in the same direction we are, or are already there. This is an eagle's flight, no chickens allowed.

Lastly, how we choose to direct our thoughts and energy is the key to whether, or how much, we believe in ourselves. The conversations we have, the television shows we watch, and what we think about on a consistent basis are all our choice. If we decide to have conversations that are mostly focused on complaining and griping, it will feed our psyche. If we keep feeding ourselves phrases like, "I'll never be able to do that" or "nobody likes me", it will become true for us.

In his book, *The Success Principles*, Jack Canfield talks about the self talk endless loop. He says our self talk reinforces our self image which determines our performance. By continually thinking and talking about the way things *are* or what you *don't like*, the more you reinforce it in your life – and so the same things keep happening. If we begin to intentionally direct our thoughts, words, and actions toward what is good, or what we *do* want to see happen, we will begin to see the change or success in our life that we have desired. Our belief in ourselves has everything to do with how we decide to think, feel, speak, and act. And yes, it is our decision.

↣ The Courage Factor

For the journey into this new chapter of life, we must toss a little courage into our backpack. Courage takes many forms. Some equate it with being a hero, or to one who is bold and adventurous. And I agree, courage is as bold as a lion, and as brave as a superhero. But as big as courage is, it is also found in the seemingly small things. For instance, to some, courage is getting out of the bed in the morning to face another day. And I can surely attest to the courage it takes some of us to say no to a slice of chocolate cake. The truth is, wherever we find it, and however we execute it, the fact that we do makes us valiant.

In Chapter 1 I shared my story of learning to do the next right thing. In my life, doing the next right thing has pretty much taken two forms. The first is "dropping out", and the next is "stepping up". When I sold my house and my car, I was definitely dropping out. I threw away the façade of being able to do it all and trying to impress the world.

Another example of dropping out is when I strategically hired someone I knew would eventually take over my role in the organization. I was in an administrative job at the time. However, by this point, I knew for certain I had to embrace my calling to teach and to write. I was reading the book *Good to Great* by Jim Collins. In his book, Jim presented a concept of "getting the right people on the bus". But before we can get the right people on the bus, we have to get the wrong people off the bus.

I really cared about the program I worked for. I was passionate about seeing it succeed. I was in an Organizational Leadership Master's degree program at the time, and I was very serious about organizational change. I embarked on a structural and job analysis for our program. I realized that in order for the program to be successful, roles needed to be reassessed, and quite frankly, some of us needed to go. It was in this phase that I recognized myself as one of those who needed to exit.

It was an interesting and sometimes uncomfortable scenario to watch unfold. As I earnestly prayed and took strategic steps, it was clear that other systems were serendipitously beginning to work in line with "my" plan. It took a lot of courage to let the plan play out. Especially because I started a ball rolling that I was not in charge of "keeping in play". In other words, I pushed the issue on the front end but I was not a controlling factor – final decision maker - in the outcomes. At the end, however, I found myself right where I dreamed of being – no longer doing administration, but teaching and writing. I think this came at least partially because of the courage and willingness to drop out.

But courage to do the next right thing is also about stepping up. We have to face the challenge of new options and opportunities. It sounds great to say that many new doors are opening but the reality is that walking through them will require some work on our part. We may have to learn new skills, create new networks, or flex a different set of discipline muscles.

The Bible tells the story of the Israelites coming into their promised land of Canaan which was referred to as "the land flowing with milk and honey". My former pastor would comment that when the Israelites finally entered the land of milk and honey, it was full of cows and bees. Whether it's a relationship, a career move, or some other new situation, it takes courage to step up and do what is required to cultivate it. It's time to step up!

In this season the courage factor is about moving on ideas - launching out! I can't help but think of the animated movie Madagascar and the lively lemurs dancing at the end. They were singing the song by musical artist, Will.I.Am, "I Like to Move

It". When I'm working on a project and ready to move an idea to the next level, I sing that song and dance around the house. You should too; or at least do something that will motivate you to get going. Many people have great ideas, and place them in a chest for safekeeping. If you are reading this book, that season is over for you. Nothing is safe in that chest - nothing. It is a burial ground for formerly great ideas. Your ideas are too amazing to die a slow, stuffy, and musty death. They must be unleashed on the world.

List Your Favorite Motivational Dance Songs Here!

1.

2.

3.

4.

5.

Don't wait for perfection; move on your ideas now. Perfection is the procrastinators dream. That is because perfection never comes. Nobody is perfect, no idea is perfect. The sooner you get your idea out there, the sooner you can receive the feedback you need to make it better. You will never know the next right thing for your project if you don't move on it.

Always look at failure as discovery. When something doesn't go as expected with your idea or project, discover what you learned from that unexpected turn of events. When things didn't go well with my gift basket business, I discovered that I liked making gift baskets as a hobby, but not really as a business. The very same year I had an unprecedented God encounter where God began to reveal to me my purpose.

Refuse to quit on your dream. Never give up unless something greater is revealed. In which case you are not giving up, you are just moving to the next level, or to a higher awareness. Have faith in God, believe in yourself, and always move forward.

Stop waiting for someone to tell you its okay to move on your dream, idea, or project. I am telling you now. But the fact that it is burning on the inside of you is proof enough that it's yours to pursue. Potential has to be "worked" out. We come to earth full of potential but if we don't do anything with it, it will never turn into purpose. If you want to find your purpose, you have to do something with your potential. All of that potential bottled up inside needs an outlet. Move it, move it!

↬ **The Creativity Factor**

Genesis 1:1-3 says, "In the beginning when God created the heavens and the earth, the earth was a formless void and darkness covered the face of the deep, while a wind from God swept over the face of the waters. Then God said, 'Let there be light'; and there was light". The first thing we should know about creativity is that it is connected to God. It is from God, and He allows it to flow through us, to bless the world.

The second thing we should remember is that creativity is connected to our voice, and to our words. In the Genesis account, everything was dark, quiet, and basically still, but as soon as God started speaking, everything awakened and became bright and lively. Creativity begins for us when we hear God speak. God spoke a word to us before time began. He downloaded it to our spirit. Once we find that file and open it, our truest creativity and purpose emerges. Now that we hear Him speaking to us, we can speak to the world. If we start speaking before God starts speaking, our words and our art are meager at best. But when we hear His voice and then share it through our unique purpose, the creativity splashes brilliantly on the canvas of life.

In this new chapter, creativity is about pulling, pushing and stretching. You must stop playing with your abilities, and hiding your light under a bushel. Now is the time to really work your purpose. Let your creativity loose by giving it a workout. Here are five factors for creativity in this season.

The first creativity factor is to **put creativity on your schedule**. Don't wait for the wind to blow a certain direction, during the full moon, in order for you to have the inspiration to work on your art. It's going to take good old fashioned discipline to perfect your craft. You must respect your art enough to create space for it. What you honor and respect grows in your life. So take out your calendar and mark off some time with your creative self. Once you set the time, keep it. Then *decide* to get into the zone. Yes, you can decide. You do not have to wait for an ominous moment of inspiration to descend from the sky. You are a walking bundle of inspiration when you stay in tune with the Holy Spirit. Remember, its God's words you need to hear before you speak (create).

The second creativity factor is to **create a lot of stuff, and create all the time**. Yes that's right, now that you have a scheduled time that cannot be broken, break into everything else on your schedule and shake it up with your creativity projects. I believe your creativity is just that important.

If you are a writer, write when you're too busy to write, write when you're relaxing on the beach, and even write when you're walking down the street. If you are a dancer, dance in the morning, dance in the evening, and even dance all day long. Find ways to do your art everywhere you are – at home, at work, in the community, on vacation.

Whatever it is you create, really put it to the test in this season. Some of what you create will be really bad. Some will be good. Some will be genius. But the less you participate in your creativity the longer it will take you to strike genius.

A fashion designer standing in front of drawings of her designs

The third creativity factor is to **trust your creative self**. Don't stifle your creativity by overloading on advice. I believe in feedback and constant improvement. However, in the midst of your creative zone is not the time to receive feedback. You want to unleash what you are hearing from God, not what you are hearing from others. Allow your uniqueness to flow, accept it, push it, pull it, stretch it, and finally embrace it.

The fourth creativity factor is to **inspire your creativity**. Don't this confused with "waiting for inspiration to inspire you" to create. This is not what I am saying here. Inspire your creativity is about the push, pull and stretch. It says, go places you don't normally go, see things you don't normally see, and make connections to your art in and around these things. It's an abstract concept to keep yourself fresh and your ideas novel. It's like a form of brainstorming or creative prompt. Now get out there and see something new!

And finally, the fifth creativity factor is to **create a reading list**. Oh come on, you know me by now. I'm not going to talk about creativity and not sneak the idea of books in there somewhere. You have to read a lot in your creative areas. Notice what people are saying and doing, and what people are not saying and doing. Capitalize on what they are not saying and doing by saying and doing it yourself.

↬ The Authenticity Factor

Competition is about being better than someone else, or at least doing everything you can to make people think you are. People strive and struggle, play tug-o-war, and jockey for position in a "dog eat dog" fight to the death, all in order to win. But I am here to say, take off your boxing gloves, because there is no contest. You are the "hands-down", all-time favorite when you walk in your authenticity. Nobody can touch you, or as 1980's rapper, M.C. Hammer would say, "U Can't Touch This". What are you talking about Joy? What is this phenomenon of authenticity? Let me first explain what authenticity is not.

- It's not saying anything you feel with lack of restraint
- It's not that you are perfect, in fact you acknowledge your imperfection as a key reason for your brilliance
- It's not a super spiritual state of spookiness where you speak in hushed tones and float as you walk down the street

Ask the same person, the same question, on different day, and the answer may change. That's how it is with authenticity. There are so many definitions or ways that people explain and see it. In these last few years, I have also added my own perspective to the pot. Here's what I know for sure. Authenticity is an inner journey that leads a person to be genuine. And by genuine I mean a bona fide, certified, first-rate version of you. Authenticity is being your highest and best version of real. The only way we can get here is by implementing the inner journey practices discussed in Chapter 3 (Compounded RSAP).

What does authenticity look like? In my study of this concept

- way of being in the world - I have observed three major things. First, an authentic person is present and connected to life in a caring way. This type of person brings one hundred percent. They offer all of who they are – body, mind, heart, spirit – to all of what they do. They are not just hearers; they are listeners, paying attention to detail and being in tune with their environment. Their response comes from a meaningful place and you can tell they are fully engaged.

Second, in an authentic person, you will find that there is a refreshing absence of any intention to deceive. These people are not interested in giving false impressions, evading questions, or giving half-truths. Another wonderful aspect is that they are not trying to gain personal advantage. Yes, that's right; they are not in competition with anyone except themselves. They know that *their* winning is not dependent upon *your* losing. In fact, they believe they win more when they help you win as well!

Third, an authentic person is comfortable in their own skin. They are not trying to be like anyone else, or trying to impress others. They know their values – the why behind what they do. The authentic person has been on a journey that allows them to

- accept themselves
- like who they are
- be at ease with who they are
- be at ease with what they bring

Authenticity is more valuable than competition, all day, and every day. If you focus on competing against others, you are taking your creative energy away from your area of genius. By doing so, you are basically giving it into the hands of your competitor. When Steve Jobs came back to Apple after some years of operating another venture, he said that too many people in the company had an attitude that thought "for Apple to win Microsoft has to lose". He then said, "That's not true. Apple just has to remember who Apple is".

The fact is if you are truly flowing in your purpose, no one can be a better version of you. So keep your focus. People can mimic you and even try to listen in on your trade secrets, but if you are your highest and best version of you, they will always come short of your unique brilliance.

Chapter 4 Reminder List:
Balance your greatness with an attitude of humility
Don't place your security in your abilities
To belittle ourselves is an insult to God
Find the strength to break away from toxic relationships
Intentionally direct your mind toward what is good
Courage can include "dropping out" or "stepping up"
Creativity begins for us when we hear God speak
Put creativity on your schedule
Be a bona fide, certified, first-rate version of you
Be at ease with what you bring to the table

INVESTIGATE NEW GOOD HABITS!

Which of the four factors (self-concept, courage, creativity, authenticity) most resonates with you, and why?

How will you begin to flex new habit muscles in those areas? List 3 specific action items.

Write your thoughts here.

> **TRY THIS!**
>
> *Take a day to visit a nearby city. Go to the museums, visit the parks, stroll through a street fair, etc. Use your experiences as a way to "inspire your creativity". Reflect on how something you experienced can impact your art.*

Milestone #4 Completion Checklist (check all that apply):
____I read this chapter
____I reflected on items relevant to my life
____I completed all of the activities in this chapter
____I visited a nearby city and inspired my creativity

Let me know how this chapter helped you and
which factor you are planning to flex more!

Send me a Facebook post at www.facebook.com/AudacityDare
Tweet me at https://twitter.com/AudacityDare
Email me at www. audacitydare.com/contact.html

Congratulations on Completing Milestone #4!

Enter Your Name Here

Great Achiever Trophy

Chapter 5
ROCK

I can see that your chapter four "workout" is starting to sculpt you for a great life!
<ins>Welcome to Chapter 5!</ins>

Topic: ROCK
Don't limit yourself in this new season, rock your flair! There is so much more to you than you have let on. It's time to let the world know who you really are and show all of the fabulous facets of you!
Now is the time to flaunt your uniqueness. What you once thought was too quirky or weird about you is now the key to your coolness. Throw those quirks around you like a superhero's cape and fly! Rock it!   -Joy Linn

---

Promise to Self
As I read this chapter, I promise to make a true effort to fully engage concepts that are relevant to my life.

I will reflect on how to add and nurture new facets of myself. I will walk consistently toward my God-given purpose.

_____
Sign Your Name Here

⇢ Rock Your Flair

What life are you waiting for? This is not a dress rehearsal. This is the only chance you will receive – on this side of eternity – to live a phenomenal life. Are you waiting until graduation, waiting until you get married, or waiting until the children go to school? Whatever you think you are waiting for, I urge you to stop waiting, and get going.

God wants to use your gifts, abilities and talents to fulfill his mission. What a privilege! The God of all creation wants to work through you, to bless the world. It can't get better than that. You have style – a way about you – that no one else has. But you have been hiding it because you think it's quirky, or not "normal". Here is a bit of good news for you. I think we have now discovered that there is no such thing as normal. How can anyone be "typical" or "regular" when each person is created with such uniqueness?

Matthew 5: 14-16 says, "You are the light of the world. A city on a hill cannot be hidden. Neither do people light a lamp and put it under a bowl. Instead they put it on its stand, and it gives light to everyone in the house. In the same way, let your light shine before men, that they may see your good deeds and praise your Father in heaven".

What God has placed inside of you was meant to be shared. The world should see your gifts in operation. That is why they are there – to attract people (to Christ, through you). As you delve into a life of dynamic adventure, find ways to use your God-given gifts, interests, and skills, so that you can rock the attraction factor. Move out of your comfort zone and breakthrough to a new normal. Below are vignettes taken from the lives of a few of my friends who are magnetically attractive for Christ.

⇢ Rock Your Faith

My girlfriends and I have had Christian brothers who lived out their faith in such a way that not only women swooned over them, but their godliness was attractive to all people. I remember the year that a group of us lived at a seminary. Our brothers made a grand entrance on Valentine's Day with flowers and candy for us.

We were all single, and none of us were dating. But our brothers wanted to make sure that we felt loved and appreciated on this special occasion.

Later that night, when I was in my room alone, I looked at my rose and candy hearts, and I cried incessantly. I knew God had orchestrated this special gesture just for me. It had come during a season when I suffered with extreme loneliness. And that particular year, the thought that I would not receive a Valentine plagued me. As God would have it, instead of not receiving a Valentine, this was actually the first Valentine's Day since college that held deep meaning for me. I believe faith is an action word. We should always be ready to move in faith and carry out even the simplest mission of God in the lives of those around us. The more we do that, the more desirable we become….to everyone.

There are also people like Taiye Oladapo. Have you ever met someone who is pleasantly serious about the Lord in everything they do – work or play? That's how I describe Taiye Oladapo. She is the type of person we all desperately need in our lives. She aspires to a passionate and genuine approach toward the study of God's Word, she is also a worshipper, and prayer warrior. But these things don't stand aloof as a religious status symbol. No, they are mingled with a true caring for people.

The thing about Taiye is, she seeks to make every encounter a God encounter for all involved. As she sows seeds of faith, she consistently watches in anticipation for the good plans of Jeremiah 29:11 to manifest. Someone once said of Taiye, "When you leave a conversation with her, you feel clean". Wow, sounds like being in the presence of Jesus! There is nothing more attractive than being genuine through and through.

A conversation entitled "Rock Your Faith" cannot end without discussing Pastor Rick Butler. Thirty-something Pastor Rick Butler is single and abstinent, and many young adults in Philadelphia who have flocked to hear him speak admire his decision to wait for marriage. Pastor Rick believes in getting the message out there about what matters most. And for him, obeying God and saving your sexuality for marriage is at the top of the list.

How many women do you think want a future husband like Pastor Rick? I would venture to say plenty. And with sexually transmitted diseases at an all time high, his message on abstinence is as timely for people in the community of faith as it is for anyone in any community. Oh yes, abstinence rocks the attraction factor!

↳ Rock Your Purpose

While some waddle around in indecisiveness there are others who are off blazing a trail. People who live out their purpose are definitely attractive. They are some of the most exciting and fascinating people. Like Shelton Mercer, COO of Stop Hunger Now and Managing Principal of Twit Change. This guy is a powerhouse! He spends his days doing social good, by helping charities and organizations do better.

Stop Hunger Now has mobilized 250,000 volunteers to package over 70 million meals, which they've delivered to 70 countries. Shelton travels the world and gets elbow to elbow in the trenches of relief work, and it inspires the heck out of me. The way he uses social media for the benefit of the most needy boggles my mind.

Twit Change has raised over $1 million via Twitter campaigns that have connected 400 celebrities, including Eva Longoria, Ryan Seacrest, and Troy Polamalu, with their fans.

The first words I said to Shelton the day I met him in person were, "Hi, you're my hero". Sure, it was a little hokey, but in that moment, I meant it with every fiber of my being. The tag line of Shelton's life, as well as his Facebook and Twitter posts is, "Live ON Purpose". And he takes that quite seriously. I think when we learn how to live on purpose our attractiveness factor soars!

And when I think about magnetic purpose, I also can't help but think of my dear friends, Carolyn and Krista. Carolyn Crouch-Robinson and Krista Wieder have committed to finding ways to live in community with total strangers. Not only that, but to bring ethnically, racially and generationally diverse people together to create lasting bonds.

They did this simply by purchasing a house, and loving and accepting all people. Sounds warm and fuzzy, but it required much prayer and patience, a willingness to be challenged, and a good amount of planning. Now they boast German exchange students, actors, authors, divorcees, graduate students, teachers, and travelers among the ranks of those who lived at their gracious home in Germantown. Attend any of their gatherings, such as the yearly Easter dinner, and you will find people reminiscing about the time they lived in the house, or affectionately referring to which room they formerly occupied.

Somehow people who normally would not meet and definitely would not be in relationship with one another find common ground within this unlikely family. Discovering what you bring to the world, and committing to bring it, will also bring the world to your front door. Now that's attraction!

↠ Rock Your Brilliance

My friend Dwaine "The Creative Brain" Vassell is super mega intelligent! He's an animator of computer generated imagery, and a science and technology buff. He reviews and ranks great animation in his field, just for fun; he talks about the solar system and stars I've never heard of; and he expresses creative ideas that are shear genius.

Dwaine is not a show off; he simply enjoys the adventure of creativity, discovery, and exploration. And he is just, well, brilliant. But if I tell Dwaine he is brilliant, he says, "All people are born brilliant". In his estimation, brilliance comes from having a strong imagination and the desire to explore and figure things out. In other words, he says, "brilliance is curiosity". If you've ever met anyone like Dwaine, you know as well as I that intelligence is definitely attractive.

Have you ever seen the slogans in public school hallways – "you have to read to lead" – and other rhyming phrases? I must admit, I never really like those signs. They always seem so unoriginal. But the truth is, too many of us do not read, and too many of us don't care to think. Why should we? Our cell phones and other electronic devices can do the thinking for us.

But people like Dwaine Vassell remind us that human imagination and creativity are priceless, and must be cultivated. It is what triggers our desire for personal development, and spurs our aspirations to research, organize, and build. In addition to his website development business, and writing his upcoming book on creativity, Dwaine is developing products and services that will benefit children. He is creating an interactive platform that brings together art, design, education, storytelling and technology.

Dwaine "The Creative Brain" Vassell is surely not wasting his space here on earth. He is filling it by using his brilliance to benefit the world. It's time to spur our creativity and intellect. Offer something better, contribute something more. Rock your brilliance…its super mega attractive!

↛ Rock Your Financial Savvy

I've been reading a personal finance blog called Budgets are Sexy – an "interesting" title. I have never been one to follow a blog consistently. Yet these articles keep me coming back for more. Financial savvy is indeed attractive.

It reminds me of my friend Ayesha Selden who is a private wealth manager. I remember our first financial meeting. She was in her twenties and very serious about financial matters. I was in my thirties and still "wishy washy" about my finances. While I was older than she, I still admired the life that Ayesha was fashioning for herself. She was clear about her direction, deliberate about her actions, a high achiever....and on top of all that, fashionable.

I'm not ashamed to say, I think I secretly wanted to be Ayesha. Some years later I see that she has stayed true to consistently building her financial empire and continues to thrive. She advises high-wealth clients, she travels and she lives a great life! Disagreements concerning money are one of the top three reasons couples split – and that is not attractive at all. For our own well being and the stability of our families, I think it's time to be financially educated and wise. Having our financial house in order definitely rocks the attraction factor.

⇥ Rock Your Good Health

Twenty-something Tia Burroughs dropped 60 pounds to rock her good health. Tired of being belittled by people and concerned about her health, Tia got serious about working out and changing her eating habits. She admits the snack foods like chips are still a nagging temptation but she realizes health is her greatest asset.

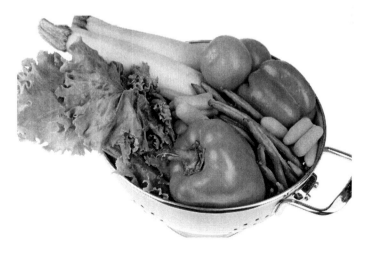

Tia loves to swim and run and wants to be able to still enjoy these things when she is in her fifties and sixties. What could be more attractive than the glow of good health? Now is the time to begin working out and eating healthy! Not only is it attractive, it is wise.

You have a lot in your uniqueness arsenal. And you have much to offer the world. You are already bold, attractive, fearless and strong. Now, how can you become more attractive – more effective for God's work? How can you strengthen your faith, live out your purpose, use your brilliance, become financially stable and be as healthy as possible? In this new chapter of your life, don't settle for the one-dimensional you. Take it to the next level and rock the full package.

Chapter 5 Reminder List:
Don't limit yourself in this new season, rock your flair
Your quirks are the key to your coolness
God wants to use you to fulfill his mission
God has given you gifts and abilities to attract people – to Him
Become magnetically attractive for Christ
Do simple things to bless those around you
Live ON Purpose
Cultivate your creativity and imagination to benefit the world
Financial savvy rocks the attraction factor
Don't settle for the one-dimensional you

INVESTIGATE UNUSED GIFTS, INTERESTS & SKILLS!

What are a few areas of flair that you can add to your life? Or, what areas have been neglected that need to be revived? Don't limit yourself to the categories listed in the chapter; reflect on your specific situation. Maybe you need to rock your smile more, your foreign language skills, or volunteerism. What steps will you take to begin? Write your thoughts here.

> # TRY THIS!
>
> *Rock your faith by doing an intentional act of kindness for someone each day this week. Why not bless your spouse, your child, your co-worker, a stranger, someone on the train, someone in line at the supermarket or at the bank, etc.*

Milestone #5 Completion Checklist (check all that apply):
____I read this chapter
____I reflected on items relevant to my life
____I completed all of the activities in this chapter
____I did a week of intentional acts of kindness…and I'm not going to stop now!

Which story did you find most interesting in this chapter? I would love to hear your thoughts about it!

Send me a Facebook post at www.facebook.com/AudacityDare
Tweet me at https://twitter.com/AudacityDare
Email me at www. audacitydare.com/contact.html

Congratulations on Completing Milestone #5!

Enter Your Name Here

You Rock! Trophy

Chapter 6
AFFIRM

I can tell that chapter five inspired you to do more with your abilities, gifts and talents!
Welcome to Chapter 6

Topic: AFFIRM

What in the world were you thinking? I actually don't have to ask that question because your life shows what direction your thoughts have taken. If you think something enough, you will eventually say it out loud, and subsequently act on it. If you are an adult, much of what you see in your life is the outcome of your past thoughts, words, and actions.

You have had great thoughts, and not so great thoughts. It's time to have way more great thoughts, which will lead to a great life. It's time to live in the affirmative, and change your mind! —Joy Linn

---

Promise to Self

As I read this chapter, I promise to make a true effort to fully engage concepts that are relevant to my life.

I will consciously seek to change ineffective thought patterns, words, and actions. I will walk consistently toward my God-given purpose.

_____

Sign Your Name Here

➢ Change Your Mind

Most people want to live a happy, meaningful, and fulfilled life. How you think, speak and act affects these possibilities. You cannot harbor mindsets that go against what you most want to see in your life. If you could just change your mind, you could change your life. For instance a small change in how you think about and handle money could eventually mean a big change in your bank account. Or, a decision to go to college and earn a degree could make all the difference in landing the job of your dreams.

Oprah said one day she asked herself what would happen if she really believed Philippians 4:13, "I can do all things through Christ which strengthens me". She decided to test it out and moved forward in her calling in life. The world now knows her great outcome. The point is, you may have to think and act differently today, to get to the place you want to be tomorrow.

So much negative self talk is swirling in your head every moment. Some of it you heard growing up and it just stuck; other things you made up along the way. In either case it is a constant barrage of thoughts that can keep you from living the great life you were meant to live. These things tell you that you are not good enough, you will never amount to anything, and you are ugly, and so on. The only way you will enter a state of clarity and purpose is if you begin to counteract those negative thoughts with good, positive, affirming thoughts. Philippians 4:8 says, "Finally, brothers, whatever is true, whatever is noble, whatever is right, whatever is pure, whatever is lovely, whatever is admirable – if anything is excellent or praiseworthy – think about such things". I am a strong proponent of affirmation and visualization. I am not ashamed to say that my thoughts need to be renewed.

⇢ Change Your View of Yourself

The story I am about to tell may not seem, at first glance, very affirming. If you are like me, when you hear the word "affirmation", you may associate it with encouragement, something beautiful to the soul, or pleasant statements we repeat to ourselves. But as I share this story, remember, that the literal definition of the word "affirm" means to declare, accept, or assert strongly and publicly.

In elementary school I was bullied. I was skinny, smart and quiet. I guess that set me up as a target. It wasn't until much later that I learned the art of preventative bluffing – acting and speaking in a tough manner so that people will not pick fights with you. Meanwhile, in elementary school, Regina consistently stole my homework answers and threatened to beat me up if I told the teacher. Marvin, who had an unsightly skin condition which caused his skin to be extremely dark and wrinkled, enjoyed calling me "blackie" and "tar baby". I was too young to realize that he was deflecting the pain of his situation on to me.

By middle school, I had gained weight. By most standards I would have been considered a bit chubby, a fact that a family member or two made sure to reinforce. I was attending a predominantly white private Christian school which at times espoused racist beliefs. It seemed that black students were always singled out for reprimand and detention. African American students who stayed after school for activities (or detention) and left school at later hours were often chased by white teenagers who lived in the neighborhood, and fights ensued.

Riding the bus home was no picnic either. African American public school students would ridicule African American students who went to private school, especially for speaking proper English. In many ways this was a very depressing time for me and all of this fed into my self-concept.

For many years I regretted the fact that I begged my parents to send me to a public high school, but I don't regret it anymore. Not going there would have only delayed the life defining moment that it produced. There I was for the first time in a public school, and a school with an all Black student population. Can you say culture shock? I may have been much bigger, but I was still a target for bullies. I'm sure people could smell fear on me when they walked by. The environment and the students were very hostile as seen through my suburban, private school eyes. It was like nothing I had ever experienced. Luckily (or so I thought) I was in a special magnet program which grouped the smart kids together for advanced classes. But I didn't anticipate homeroom, gym, the hallways, and the bathroom where the student body was integrated. These were possible death zones.

I spent most of 9th grade at Poochie's house, on McMahon Street, for of fear of a 12th grade bully who constantly threatened to beat me up. Poochie's was the local "hookey house" where many kids hung out, after his mom went to work. Sometimes I couldn't believe I was there. I was such an obedient child, and I absolutely loved learning, but I feared being beat up more. I was trapped, and breaking the rules was the only alternative. So there I was, with my new friends and thinking, "I guess this is my life now". But in the spring of my ninth grade year something interesting happened.

Unprotected and scared for my life, a girl picked a fight with me in the girl's locker room after gym class. This was one of the few times I decided to show up to the "death zone" for gym, and sure enough a near death experience arose. It was spring and I had gone through almost a whole school year of dodging bullies and thugs. And now here I was, confronted.

Something inside of me must have snapped because I began shouting at the girl, and going ballistic. I said, "Oh, you want to fight me" and "you think you can beat me"? I just kept mouthing off and wouldn't stop. Then two things happened. First, I could see the girl was getting scared. Second, I saw the gym teacher from afar coming our way, so I knew I wasn't going to die. The stars had aligned, this was my moment and I had better seize it. I really ramped up the hype talk and actually moved in close to the girl's face. I was loud and crazy.

Of course the gym teacher arrived and broke it up, but by that time, without ever laying a hand on the girl, I was the winner of the fight. Why? Because I was the loudest, the boldest, and seemingly fearless and she was backing down. Little did I know that this would become a life defining moment for me – it would be the moment I first changed my view of myself. It was in that moment that I *affirmed* the new me for that era. I *declared and asserted publicly* some things about myself that day. Here is what really happened.

I WENT FROM	TO
I am scared to death	I am fearless
I'm frustrated	I am encouraging myself
Why did I come to this school	I control my experience
My life is horrible	I set the tone for my life
I'm stuck	I create my reality

While the method of getting there could be debated, it still remains that this was a very important win in my life. I realized that how I think, speak, and act affects my success.

➢ Change Your View of Failure

I have failed many times, at many things, and yet I live with no regrets. I have learned not to take myself so seriously, and not to believe that I am defined by my mistakes. Proverbs 24:16 says, "For though a righteous man falls seven times, he rises again…" I am defined more by my resilience than by my failures. It's the ability to learn from mistakes and keep going that makes you a winner. You have to learn how to fail forward, or fail into your success. When you get stuck and wallow in your mistakes you lose. Always learn the lessons and keep it moving!

Failures are a key way to find out who you are and who you are not. But when you fail, you have to ask yourself some questions to get to the bottom of the issue. Here are a few questions to ask:

- What happened?
- What did I expect to happen?
- How did I contribute to what happened?
- What could I have done differently that would have given a better outcome?
- Have I answered all of these questions truthfully?

I honestly think there is too much taboo around failure. As human beings it comes with the package. This doesn't mean that we go around failing for failures sake. But we also shouldn't treat it as though it is the end of the world. In fact, many times it signifies a bright and brand new start. I don't even think of my failures as failures anymore. I learn so much from them and have grown to realize they are inextricably tied to my success.

↣ Change What You Will Accept from Yourself

There were things in my life that were fuzzy, mediocre or just plain unacceptable. A new mind meant I wasn't going to accept these things any longer. I decided that I was going to really love God, really love others, and really love myself. I was affirming the best in me.

I've been in church all of my life. My parents took me there as an infant, and it shaped the entirety of my life – the good, the bad and the ugly. But here's the thing, my religious roots made me a religious person. In some ways this can be good, in other ways it is not. There is a form of religion that moves us away from God. It seems honorable, industrious and dutiful but is actually rooted in ego serving and selfishness.

When I began to change my mind, I changed my connection with God from religious, to relationship. The reality is that when I was focused on being religious, my relationship with God was limited. There was church attendance, a few formulated prayers, and acts of service. Now I am serious, and God and I talk all day long because we are in a love relationship.

I always want to share things with God and also hear what he has to say. And sometimes I sit with him and we don't say anything, we just enjoy each other's presence. It feels good to know he's right there.

When you are in love, everything starts to revolve around your relationship. That's how it is with me and God. My whole life is wrapped up in his person and his mission. I had to sit with him and find my true purpose. Now our lives are so entwined because we are walking hand in hand to carry out his vision. My new mindset refuses to have anything less than God's entire plan for my life.

When I decided I was going to really love God that automatically meant that I was going to really love others. How can we love God who we have not seen when we do not love our brother? (1

John 4:20) But because we are so trained to wear masks and play games, authenticity can be extremely hard. I guess because of fear and other distractions, people constantly dodge being real with those they care about. Who ever thought that just being yourself would end up being so difficult?

When I changed my mind I decided I was going to really love people. I recognized that it might look weird but I was willing to take the risk. I became ok with the fact that I really cared. And you know what I found out? When people see that you are genuine, they are more than okay with you caring about them as well.

I also love myself, yes I do. I am Gods fearfully and wonderfully made creation. As such I am committed to nurturing myself in body, soul and spirit. In the past I treated my body poorly. In recent years I decided to nurture my body by increasing healthy habits and decreasing poor habits. Instead of processed foods, I eat more homemade foods made with fresh ingredients. Fruit and veggies are abundant in my eating plan. I also drink large amounts of the best water available and I exercise regularly in locations with fresh air, sun and water.

Nurturing my soul is vitally important to me. Everyone does this differently, but I do this mostly through reading, writing, reflection and meaningful conversation. Lastly, prayer and worship nurture my spirit. The inner rush of glory that it brings provides the insight, faith, hope, love and joy that keep me on mission every day.

↠ Change What You Will Create in Your Life

When I first hit the adult scene I was pretty much on the track to create nothing but a mess in my life. By the time I was 23 I had done that pretty well, and then I was promoted and on my way to creating a wreck.

In my youth, I always had a sense of wanting to create some type of change in the world to make things better. At five I wanted to create art (finger paintings) so that people could have something beautiful to look at. At ten I wanted to end racism. By the time I was sixteen I was fixated with creating social systems – schools, clinics, prisons - that would more adequately serve the poor, while allowing them to maintain their dignity.

But it really wasn't until much later in my adulthood that I took the time to self-assess. That's when I truly knew what I was meant to create in the world. Self-assessment is looking at you and evaluating the landscape. It requires that we think about, speak to, and interact with ourselves. That may sound a bit crazy, but in essence this is what is needed to get to a deeper understanding of who we really are.

Out of my self-assessment I began to recognize that I was meant to create encounters, experiences, and moments that would propel people into a great life. My mission is to inspire and motivate utilizing various modes of communication including books, classes, daily conversations and interactions, meetings, seminars, etc.

One of the most empowering things you can do after a time of self-assessment is to create a personal mission statement. When I wrote my personal mission statement it solidified for me who I wanted to be in the world, and how I would go about being it. Now this statement is the guide that keeps me moving in my purpose, and consistently creating.

Chapter 6 Reminder List:
If you can change your mind, you can change your life
Think positive, affirming thoughts
To affirm means to declare, accept, or assert strongly and publicly
Affirm the new you for this era
Learn from mistakes and keep moving forward
Get rid of mediocre thinking and living – be "all in"
Really love God, really love others, and really love yourself
Use self-assessment to know what you are meant to create in life
Self-assessment is looking at you, and evaluating the landscape
Write a personal mission statement

INVESTIGATE WAYS YOU CAN CHANGE!

Have you ever had a life defining moment that caused you to change your view of yourself? How exactly did your thoughts about yourself change? Write your story here.

> **TRY THIS!**
> *Spend some time this week writing a personal mission statement. Check my website for samples!*
> *www.AudacityDare.com*

Milestone #6 Completion Checklist (check all that apply):
____I read this chapter
____I reflected on items relevant to my life
____I completed all of the activities in this chapter
____I wrote my personal mission statement

I am always happy to hear your ideas, feedback and thoughts!

Send me a Facebook post at www.facebook.com/AudacityDare
Tweet me at https://twitter.com/AudacityDare
Email me at www. audacitydare.com/contact.html

Congratulations on Completing Milestone #6!

Enter Your Name Here

You're a Winner! Trophy

A Word on Affirmation & Visualization

It is a good practice to affirm positive and productive thoughts and ideas in our minds. I've said it before and I'll say it again, I am the prophet of my life. I believe in speaking prophetically over myself. And you are the prophet of your life as well. You have the ability to encourage yourself with your thoughts and words just as you would say kind things to others. You are worth it. Particularly since about 80% of self talk is negative, if you want to break through barriers to your best success, you have to flood out the old negative messages that stay on repeat in your head. The only way to do that is to replace it with new thoughts that are leading you in the direction you want to go.

I have heard people say, "I've tried affirmations, and that stuff doesn't work". In one sense they are right. Just saying the words is not going to make it happen. You have to set your mind, heart and emotions to believe it. God has called us to live a life of faith. In fact without faith, the Bible says it is impossible to please God (see Hebrews 11:6). When God spoke creation into existence He didn't stand there and say, ok so I'm going to say these words and see if anything happens. No, He fully expected what He said to occur, and it did.

When you say your affirmations, really mean it deep down, and express it with that same depth of feeling and meaning. Have you ever heard the phrase, "he wanted to win so bad he could taste it"? That's how speaking our affirmations should be. The thing we are expecting is not fully actualized but we are still currently experiencing it as though it were. That's just ridiculous you say. Why, yes it is! Are you literally crazy enough to believe in your destiny, your dream, your great life, your purpose, your mission in life? I am.

Lastly, I believe affirmation and visualization are connected. Once we speak something we have to begin to see it even though no one else can, and up until everyone else can. In 1 Kings 17-18 there was a drought which God used Elijah to pronounce over the land, due to the evilness of King Ahab. Elijah said there would be no rain in the land until he spoke it.

Three years later, he sensed God telling him to speak to Ahab again, to tell him it was going to rain. After he spoke these words, Elijah went into deep prayer, and then told his servant to go look toward the sea for signs of rain. His servant came back and said he saw nothing. Elijah asked him to do this seven times before his servant came back with the report of seeing a cloud the size of a man's hand. Elijah was assured that it was going to rain, even when there was no physical evidence of its appearance. His servant most likely thought he was crazy. But it was so real to Elijah, not only could he could see it but the Bible says he could hear the sound of abundant rain. And he kept his servant going back until he was able to visualize it too.

I believe affirmation and visualization is so important to your success that I am including a few affirmation cards here in the book for your use. Cut them out and take them along with you or just flip through the pages of the book during free moments in your day.

AFFIRMATIONS FOR ATTITUDE & PERSPECTIVE

I am gratefully choosing joy today! I am smiling brightly and causing other people to smile and have a great day.

I am so grateful that God is living inside of me; with Him, I am accomplishing great things!

I am so grateful that love is pouring out of me and I am helping and healing others.

I am so grateful that I am producing great results. It feels wonderful being so productive everyday!

I am so thankful that I am using my gifts and talents and blessing people all over the world!

I am so happy that I am living every moment to the fullest and giving God the glory!

I am so grateful that I am accessing everything I need to fulfill my purpose.

I am so thankful that I am motivating others to live a great life!

I am so grateful that ways are being made for me to carry out my calling.

AFFIRMATIONS FOR POSITIVE SELF CONCEPT

> Woo hoo! I love being uniquely beautiful and gifted! Thank you Lord!

> I love having so much creativity; ideas are constantly flowing my way!

> I am so grateful that I am constantly growing in good attributes, more and more each day.

> Yes! It feels so empowering that I am consistently flowing in courage and strength to fulfill my purpose!

> I am enjoying being thoughtful and kind. It feels so good that I am respecting others and they feel valued.

> I feel so wonderful being diligent and conscientious every day, it adds such meaning to my life!

AFFIRMATIONS FOR PROGRESS

I am so grateful that my life is lining up with the great plans God has for me!

I am so thankful that I am making great progress and steadily moving forward!

I am so grateful that I am enjoying focusing on the projects set before me and that I am completing them with excellence.

I am so grateful that I am often discovering new abilities and strengths.

I am so thankful that I am consistently growing in knowledge, understanding and wisdom.

I am so grateful that I am practicing good habits that are yielding great results in my life.

I am so grateful that I am completing with ease the items I started.

I am so thankful that I am constantly improving in every way and always getting better and better.

AFFIRMATIONS FOR SUCCESS

I am so grateful that I am accomplishing everything God desires me to accomplish today.

I am grateful that I am exampling what success looks like!

I am so grateful that I am winning today and everyday!

I am so excited that I am carrying out my purpose everyday!

I am so thankful that I am thinking big and achieving my goals.

I am so grateful that I am winning awards, prizes and other commendation in my areas of expertise.

I am so grateful that I am receiving lucrative contracts every year.

I am so thankful that I am enjoying the excellent opportunities that I am receiving today.

I am so grateful that opportunities are abounding for me!

I am so excited that great success follows me wherever I go.

> I am so grateful that every situation is working in my favor.

> I am so grateful that I have the audacity to succeed!

AFFIRMATIONS FOR BIG THINGS

I am so amazed and grateful that my life is encouraging others to step up and do great things for God.

I am so pleased that all of my projects are receiving the green light and are moving forward with ease.

I am so thankful that God is using me to pour out loads of blessing on people all over the world!

AFFIRMATIONS FOR MEANING IN LIFE

I am so grateful that I am learning to hold every moment as sacred in God's plan for my life.

It feels so wonderful that I am allowing the help, hope, and love I need in my life to enter in.

I am so grateful that I am using out-of-the-box thinking and that I am accomplishing my greatest dreams!

AFFIRMATIONS FOR A BETTER LIFESTYLE

I am so grateful that I am living a life of financial freedom.

I am so grateful that I am living and working in a pleasant environment every day.

I am so thankful that I am achieving success doing what I love.

Everyday Can Be a Day at the Beach!

I grew up loving the beach. When I became an adult it was the only place I would run to for solitude. It was my special place of reflection. There I was always sure to find clarity. At some point however, I began to question why I had to journey to the beach in order to have such great clarity and soul peace. As I mulled over my thoughts, I realized I could actually have this same reflective experience on a regular basis, without necessarily hearing seagulls and digging my feet in the sand. When I schedule times of reflection into my weekly schedule, suddenly a routine day can become a day at the beach.

I am adding a few more reflection activities here to keep you growing in your times of solitude. I want you to reflect and keep reflecting, self assess and keep self assessing, pray and keep praying. As life moves on we change. Compounded RSAP is about growing with the change and consistently knowing who you are, where you are, and what you're thinking in deep and meaningful ways.

TEN CLOSE-TO-HOME PLACES TO SIT AND REFLECT

1. Bedroom
2. Bathroom
3. Garden
4. Hammock
5. Park
6. Library
7. Zoo
8. Museum
9. Bookstore
10. Café
11. _____ (add places you find)
12. _____
13. _____
14. _____
15. _____

YOUR "IF ONLY" STORY

Get a few sheets of blank paper (Note: do not complete this exercise in your journal, use separate sheets of paper). On each sheet write one of your prominent "if only" stories. The "if only" story is that phrase that holds us back from our success. It keeps us in a dream state, never to awaken to the great life we were meant to live. They sound like this:

> If only I could lose weight I would get a promotion
> If only I had more money I would be able to....
> If only I didn't have kids....

Reflect on ways you can breakthrough your "if only's". How can you face the fact that they are merely excuses and begin to take action to defeat the things that have held you back? Do you need a healthy eating plan, a workout plan, personal coaching to gain confidence, a second job to make more money, etc.? Reflect and discover concrete ways to move toward success in incremental ways.

Once you have written your new action plan in your journal, rip up each sheet of paper that had an "if only" statement on it. Throw these away!

FINE LINE BETWEEN LOVE AND HATE

What is one thing you love to do so much you would do it without getting paid? Have people ever told you that you do a good job with that thing? If so, this could be a clue to your purpose. Also, what is something that you hate or something that grates against your nerves? Does homelessness, racism, or no community center in your neighborhood make you angry? This can also be a clue to a problem you are meant to help solve, or a mission that you are meant to give your life to serving. Reflect and journal on your most passionate loves and hates.

START A PURPOSE EXPERIMENT BOOK CLUB

One of the best ways to deeply reflect on something is to be able to have conversation about it with others. Tell your friends and family about *The Purpose Experiment* and encourage them to read it together along with you. Now that you have read it (or even if you have not) you can be the facilitator for the book club. Get together at a local bookstore or at someone's home to discuss and share. Re-reading the material will reinforce the lessons for you, and you will see things you did not notice in your first reading. You will also be able to reflect on your life in new ways, as well as introduce those close to you to a life changing experience! You can find ideas for how to start a book club on my website www.AudacityDare.com

QUESTIONS, QUESTIONS & MORE QUESTIONS

A good way to reflect and self-assess is to just ask interesting or unique questions. Remember as you answer the questions to "dig into the question of why" (Chapter 2). Here are a few to get you started:

What is one word that best describes you?

What are your three favorite books of all time?

What is one thing you wish you had done but never did?

Think of a time you felt best about yourself (not the big flashy times like a wedding or the birth of a child, but something more common yet significant). What were you doing? Where were you? Who were you with? Journal about these times referring to why they were and are significant.

PERSONALITY ASSESSMENTS

If you have never taken a personality assessment or have not completed one in many years, try it! These assessments help us understand our personality and preferences in deeper ways. It's actually pretty amazing. I have found it to be a very helpful step in discovering my purpose. A well known personality assessment is the Meyers Briggs Type Indicator (MBTI). Usually these assessments are given in professional settings, but you can find shorter versions online that will at least give you a brief taste. The Personality Pathways website might be a good place to start. http://www.personalitypathways.com/type_inventory.html

CREATE YOUR OWN AFFIRMATION CARDS

The affirmation cards in this book are just a start. Buy some 3x5 cards and write your own personalized affirmations. What good things do you need to see more of in your life? What areas do you need serious personal growth? Write what you want to see in the form of an affirmation. The key is to write it in the present tense, as if you are currently enjoying it in your life.

REINVENT YOURSELF

Is what you really want to be and do in life locked away in some deep cavern of your soul longing to be free? Unleash it today! If your inside and your outside don't match, you are most likely adding tremendous stress to your daily life. The first step is to change your mind. Someone probably told you that you couldn't do or be that thing. But if after deep prayer and reflection you believe you are meant to be it, erase the negative script by writing a new script for yourself – the I CAN script. Make use of research to help you with knowing the steps required to reach your goal -in other words, Google it. Reflect and journal about the steps necessary to get you from where you are, to where you want to be. Then take steps each day toward the new you!

I share new activities on my website often, check regularly at www.AudacityDare.com

A Final Word to My Readers

At some point, I decided to be in love. I was not in a romantic relationship, but I decided to really love life. I decided to love God and people. I decided to re-create what I did for a living. I decided to go after my goals. In short, I decided to dare myself to live a great life. Here's to you appreciating who you are, what you have, and why you were born. Here's to you pushing the boundaries, coloring outside the lines and challenging yourself. Here's to you living life with meaning, purpose, gusto and moxie. Here's to you falling in love!

Step 1: STOP destructive and self-defeating behaviors

Step 2: LOOK at the lessons your life is revealing

Step 3: LISTEN to God

Step 4: FLEX new good habits and practices

Step 5: ROCK your God-given gifts, interests and skills

Step 6: AFFIRM a new mindset

Result: Live a great life!

Now Available
The first book of the new Purpose Deck series!

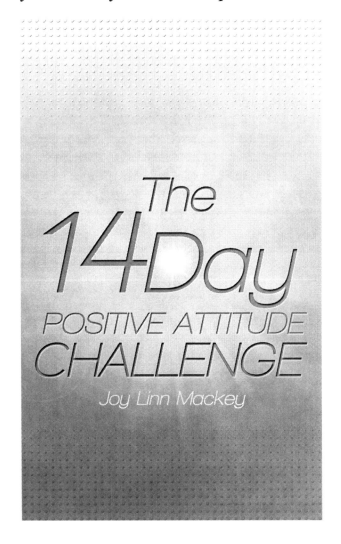

Intentionally practice life with a positive attitude!

Available online at www.AudacityDare.com

JOY LINN MACKEY

Contact me for speaking engagements, to share updates on your life, comments on the book, etc.

Send me a Facebook post at www.facebook.com/AudacityDare
Tweet me at https://twitter.com/AudacityDare
Email me at www. audacitydare.com/contact.html

CPSIA information can be obtained at www.ICGtesting.com
Printed in the USA
BVOW030110011112
304293BV00001B/4/P